# DAVE GAHAN
DEPECHE MODE & THE SECOND COMING

Published in 2009 by
INDEPENDENT MUSIC PRESS
Independent Music Press is an imprint of I.M. P. Publishing Limited
This Work is Copyright © I. M. P. Publishing Ltd 2009

*Dave Gahan – Depeche Mode & The Second Coming*
by Trevor Baker

All Rights Reserved

This book is sold subject to the condition that it shall not, by way of trade or otherwise, be lent, re-sold, hired out or otherwise circulated without the publisher's prior consent in any form of binding or cover other than that which it is published and without a similar condition being imposed on the subsequent purchaser.

No part of this publication may be reproduced, stored in a retrieval system, or transmitted in any form or by any means, electronic, mechanical, photocopying, recording or otherwise, without the prior permission of the copyright owner.

British Library Cataloguing-in-Publication Data.
A catalogue for this book is available from The British Library.
ISBN: 978-1-906191-11-5

Cover Design by Fresh Lemon.
Cover photograph by Alexandre De Brabant/Rex Features.

Printed in the Malta.

**Independent Music Press**
**P.O. Box 69,**
**Church Stretton, Shropshire**
**SY6 6WZ**
*Visit us on the web at: www.impbooks.com*
*and www.myspace.com/independentmusicpress*
For a free catalogue, e-mail us at: info@impbooks.com
Fax: 01694 720049

# Dave Gahan

*Depeche Mode & The Second Coming*

by Trevor Baker

*Independent Music Press*

# AUTHOR'S ACKNOWLEDGEMENTS

The author would like to thank the following people for the original and exclusive interviews conducted for this book:

BJ Cole (session musician on *Songs Of Faith And Devotion*); Brian Griffin (album sleeve photographer); Dave Clayton (keyboard player on *Ultra* and member of Bomb The Bass); Peter Care (video director); Ken Thomas (producer of Dave Gahan's solo album *Paper Monsters*); Russell Lee (early promoter and fan); Rusty Egan (musician and promoter); Shaun de Feo (engineer on *Songs Of Faith And Devotion*); Steafan Hannigan (session musician on *Songs Of Faith And Devotion*); Terry Murphy (promoter and owner of The Bridgehouse venue).

# NOTE FROM THE PUBLISHER

During the production of this biography, Dave Gahan was diagnosed and then treated for a malignant tumour. Given this is an unofficial and unauthorised book, with no official involvement from Dave Gahan or Depeche Mode, the publisher – Independent Music Press – will be donating 25 pence from every copy sold to Cancer Research UK, as a gesture of goodwill.

# CONTENTS

| | | |
|---|---|---|
| Introduction | | 7 |
| 1 | Essex Boy | 9 |
| 2 | Essex Band | 16 |
| 3 | *Speak And Spell* | 27 |
| 4 | Don't Go | 35 |
| 5 | *A Broken Frame* | 45 |
| 6 | Reconstruction | 51 |
| 7 | Reward | 57 |
| 8 | Consolidation | 69 |
| 9 | Celebration | 77 |
| 10 | *Music For The Masses* | 86 |
| 11 | *Violator* | 96 |
| 12 | World Violation | 103 |
| 13 | Isolation | 111 |
| 14 | Devotion | 116 |
| 15 | Destruction | 128 |
| 16 | Desolation | 138 |
| 17 | Rehabilitation | 148 |
| 18 | Clean | 155 |
| 19 | *Paper Monsters* | 163 |
| 20 | Reunion | 173 |
| 21 | *Hourglass* | 187 |
| 22 | Around The Universe | 192 |
| Discography | | 200 |

# INTRODUCTION

In the 1980s, when Depeche Mode were seen by many, particularly in the UK, as merely a slightly odd teeny pop band, Dave Gahan must have dreamed of the day when his image would change. People would at last see the rock star not terribly well hidden behind his fresh face and a million geeky photo shoots, frilly shirts and bad suits. Well, he got what he wanted. Thanks to a well-documented and harrowing personal meltdown plus a series of searingly honest interviews he gave in the mid-1990s, Dave Gahan did indeed gain a new image.

As one of rock's most famed near-casualties.

However, the truth about Dave Gahan is that he was always a more complicated character than the stereotypically excessive rock behemoth or a frontman who only sings other people's songs. At one of his numerous nadirs, Dave Gahan famously "died" for two minutes in the back of an ambulance; yet through his fabled work with Depeche Mode, his own acclaimed solo albums and his legendary live performances, his life will always be about so much more than that.

This book is inevitably a tale of what global success can do to you, but it's also a story about what happens afterwards and how personal and professional triumph can be grasped from the edge of an abyss.

# 1
# ESSEX BOY

If Depeche Mode's early press was to be believed, it sometimes seemed like there was something astonishing about a band coming from Basildon, Essex. Basildon's not a slum. It's a perfectly normal, working-class town in south-east England. But the fact that three of the four long-term members came from there shaped how they were perceived for at least the first ten years of their career. When a band like The Smiths successfully captured a certain sound of Manchester in the 1980s, they were lauded for it. In contrast, any trace of Basildon detected in Depeche Mode's music was a cause for mass sniggering in the British press. Perhaps it's the fact that it has relatively little history: it was created as a new town in the 1940s for the nouveau-not-terribly-riche. After the Second World War, the government had ordered the creation of a 'green belt' around London, to prevent the capital swallowing the countryside whole. So, with no new houses being built in London, hundreds of thousands of people ended up in new towns on the other side of the green belt. At the time it represented the hope of a better future. It would be a better place for the baby boomers – or so planners hoped – than the bombed-out terraces that many families came from. There were new factories opening, like the giant Ford plant in nearby Dagenham. There were also good transport links to London, just 26 miles away. The town still had a green, semi-rural feel and yet it was virtually a suburb of the capital.

Dave Gahan was the first member of the band to arrive there, in 1965, when he was just three years old. His mother was Sylvia Gahan, a ticket inspector on the buses, and his father was Jack Gahan, who worked in the offices of Shell Oil. He had an older sister, Sue, and two younger brothers, Philip and Peter. Jack played the saxophone in a Big Band so Dave's early years were soundtracked by jazz, by Jack's own playing and records by the likes of Miles Davis and John Coltrane.

## DAVE GAHAN

As Sue got older, Dave was also exposed to the kind of music she liked, soul singers such as Barry White and bands like the Stylistics. There were also regular plays for his mum's favourites including sugary crooners like Johnny Mathis. Dave was a cheeky, happy child who liked to make his aunts laugh with his mimicry of rock stars like Mick Jagger.

Tragically, though, in 1972 Jack Gahan suddenly died. It goes without saying that this was a huge emotional blow for the whole family but there was a further level of confusion for Sue and David. The young Dave then learnt that his mum had been married before and that parternship had broken down, but not until after Dave had been born; therefore, her former husband, Len, was actually Dave's biological father. Things were turned upside down in an instant.

"There was always distrust for people you were meant to feel safe with after that," he said to the *Daily Mirror* in 2003. "Teachers, getting into trouble with the police. I'm still a bit like that. I'll still choose to cut through the prickly bushes rather than go down the smooth road."

It was understandably difficult for Sylvia to make ends meet, but even though Dave later remembered standing in the school dinners queue with free meal tickets, he says that his mum always protected them from any real feeling of poverty.

This was despite the fact that the well-intentioned work of the urban planners who'd created Basildon was now starting to look a little misguided. The concrete was cracking and, as the economy plummeted in the 1970s, there were not enough jobs for all the people who'd flocked there. Much of the green space had been swallowed up and there was little for kids to do. Where once there had been fields, football pitches, cricket ovals, countryside, there was now a huge town with not many jobs, and young people with nothing to do.

Dave Gahan started getting into trouble, first at home and then with the police. He began drinking and taking soft drugs at a very early age, even necking some of the barbiturates that his mum was prescribed for her epilepsy. "These little downers were where it all started," he told *NME* years later.

His escapades were mostly limited to petty vandalism; to begin with, the police would just give him warnings but this didn't deter him and he kept getting caught. It didn't help that one of his favourite activities was graffiti and he used his own name as a tag. "There weren't too many Gahans in the whole of England, never mind Basildon," he told the *The Times* in 2001. "I was arrested a fair few times. Not a very good villain."

Like most teenagers, Dave wanted to be liked and he desperately wanted to be cool. It helped that he was increasingly popular with the local girls. When he got older he would become a well-known face in the trendier Basildon pubs like The Sherwood. By this point music was already starting to become the most important thing in his life. To begin with, it was all about David Bowie, Slade and Gary Glitter. Then in 1976 and 1977 he was swept up in the new punk scene that was taking off across the country.

"I remember my mother being so outraged when the Sex Pistols cursed on TV," he told *Rolling Stone*. "I think that's really what got me going: I realised there was something I could join in with that would really piss my mum off."

He started going to see bands regularly, he got a job working on the speedway at a fairground, and he got his first tattoo done, at the age of 14, on the Southend seafront from an old sailor called Clive.

His bad behaviour persisted and eventually he'd graduated to stealing cars. He wasn't particularly any better at that than he had been as a graffiti artist and his mum had the painful task of dealing with the police every time they came round.

"I put my mum through a rough time," he said to Stephen Dalton in *Uncut*. "It was petty crap – driving and taking away, criminal damage, theft. My mum did the best she could if the law would show up. I remember one time when this police car pulled up outside. She said, 'Is it for you?' and I said 'Yes.' I distinctly remember her saying, 'David's been in all night.' But I'd written my name on a wall in paint!"

He ended up in juvenile court and eventually he was warned that he wasn't far off from a spell in a young offender's institute. "It got to the point where we'd steal cars from garages, drive them around for a bit, leave them in a field somewhere and set them alight," he told *The Observer*. "I felt I was always running from somebody, running from the law and most of the time getting caught. By the time I was 14 I'd been caught three times and a cop told me I could go down. The thought of that really horrified me but I was lucky, I got off with an attendance centre."

The "attendance centre" was in nearby Romford. It was a place of rigorous, quasi-military discipline. They made him get a haircut, taught him to box and got him working. Yet around 17 he first flirted with serious disaster at a squat party in King's Cross, London. Although he'd dabbled with relatively soft drugs before, that night somebody gave him heroin. He had no idea what it was, merely thinking that it looked a weird colour for the more usual drug, speed. "I was violently ill and passed out," he said to *The Guardian* later. "I remember thinking at the time that wasn't the drug for me."

As a hugely social person, he was always very influenced by the people around him. He liked to feel like one of the crowd. At the time his best friend was a guy called Mark. "We did everything together – got into trouble together, pulled girls together, shared girlfriends," he enthused in an interview with *No 1* magazine.

But he later said that one experience with Mark made a more lasting impression on him. He was at a party with his girlfriend when he realised that he hadn't seen either her or his best mate for a long time. "Everyone was looking at me," he told *Q*. "They knew. I pushed open the bedroom door and there's Mark's white arse bouncing up and down. That was my first reality check. It set me on this idea that I'm not good enough. I've been battling it ever since."

Fortunately, his increasing infatuation with punk was starting to make him think that being a musician wasn't as unrealistic as he'd once thought. It was when he saw The Clash for the first time that he really became inspired. He'd been into The Damned first, joining their fan-club, but The Clash made him feel that he could go beyond imitating his idols and do it himself. He started singing with different bands, including one called The Vermin who were supposed to be Basildon's answer to the Sex Pistols but none of the musicians he was playing with proved to have sufficient drive. Punk had inspired them all to think that anybody could be in a band but they hadn't realised how much dedication and effort it took.

But by the time he was 17 he was already starting to grow up. In January 1979 he met Joanne Fox, a friend of a schoolmate, at a Damned gig. By August they would be dating and by November they were inseparable. He'd already been through a lot for a 17-

year-old and, at that early age, was already thinking about putting his early wildness behind him.

Meanwhile, on the other side of Basildon's tracks, another band, Composition Of Sound, was just starting out. Consisting of Martin Gore, his best friend Andy Fletcher and another school friend, Vince Martin, they were living a very different kind of life to Dave. While Dave spent his weekends in London clubs or following punk bands to Chelmsford or Southend, Martin, Andy and Vince were all members of the local church. They didn't do drugs and Martin entirely swore off alcohol between the ages of 16 and 18. They were quiet, disciplined and studious. Everything that Dave seemingly wasn't. Vince, in particular, knew exactly what he was going to do with his life. He was going to be a musician. The only problem was that he couldn't see himself as a frontman and the other candidates, the painfully shy Martin, and Andy, who didn't want to sing, were even less likely. "We realised early on we needed a frontman," Vince said later. "Somebody who could leap about and make us look interesting."

Dave, meanwhile, had no clear idea of what he was going to do with his life. For him singing was mostly just something he did for a laugh. He liked hanging out with bands and he sometimes used to help Martin Gore's other band, French Look, with their equipment but he wasn't in any serious group himself. However, one day when some of French Look were rehearsing at Woodlands School in Basildon, they got him to join them jamming through David Bowie's 'Heroes'. In the room next door, Composition Of Sound were also trying to rehearse but they were impressed by the rough-cut vocals they could hear coming from the next room. Dave would admit later that there had been several people singing but when Vince asked him he said, "Yeah, that was me!"

It wasn't as if they were purely interested in him for his voice anyway. He took his image far more seriously than they did. He would wear black leathers, spend hours making his hair spiky, or putting it into a sleek quiff. He was already a frontman in the making.

Vince later gave Dave a call and asked him to come for an audition. They gave him three songs to sing, two of Vince's own and one by Bryan Ferry. He struggled with the originals but when they heard his smooth baritone on the Ferry track they decided that he'd got what it took. It wasn't just that he was a great singer and that he looked right, he had the kind of outgoing personality that they needed, too. He was already known as a "face" around Essex. They'd all read about the punk rock scene and the new clubs full of glamorous freaks with made-up faces. Dave had actually been to them. He seemed almost intimidatingly cool.

Dave readily agreed to join Composition Of Sound. The bands he'd been with in the past had just rehearsed in garages, getting nowhere, and his first question to Vince and Martin was, "Have you got any gigs?" When he was told they had, that sealed it. And Dave brought a lot more to the band than just a voice and a name. He knew all kinds of people and, crucially, most of them were the kind of kids who went to gigs. He had a big group of friends who used to hang out in Southend and they provided a ready-made audience of thirty or so people for the new band.

Nevertheless, right from the start, the band was a strange alliance. Vince was fiercely driven. While the rest of them took it for granted that they needed to get some kind of stable employment, he used to save up his unemployment benefit to spend on the band. He lived and breathed music and was something of a loner. Martin was the dreamer. On the surface he lived a life of perfect conformity, going to church and working in a bank as soon as he left school. Underneath, though, he had dreams and ambitions that he hadn't yet spoken to anybody about. Fletch was mates with Martin and he joined his friend in the band. He was often regarded as a professorial character, mostly because he wore glasses but in reality his was the voice of sturdy common sense in the band – a vital contribution.

Although they were very different characters, they were, in their own strange way, a *gang*. Dave's arrival changed everything. They were the kind of people that he would never have hung out with if he hadn't been in a band with them. He had a wide circle of friends and prided himself in his ability to get on with everybody, but the rest of the band were relatively 'uncool'. While all but Vince went straight out of school and into white-collar jobs, Dave's future looked more uncertain.

It was just as well he had the band because his early attempts at employment had not been a success. He once estimated that he'd had something like twenty jobs in six months, sweeping floors in a supermarket, working in offices or on building sites. In a bid to sort himself out and get a 'proper' career, he applied for a job at North Thames Gas as an apprentice fitter. He got through the initial selection procedures and was shortlisted for an interview but he knew his past behaviour might be a problem. His probation officer advised him to tell the truth but, inevitably, he didn't get the job. It was a worrying portent of what would happen if he didn't get his life together. At this point, at the end of the 1970s, with unemployment rocketing, this was a big deal.

He reluctantly decided to go back into education, enrolling at Southend Art College to study window design. His only qualifications were in art and technical drawing so it seemed like the logical choice.

It's significant that when he went to art school it wasn't with the intention of studying fine art and hiding from the world of work for a few years, as so many other pop stars had done before him. He wasn't from that kind of background. He enrolled in a course with a job at the end of it because the idea of making a living out of music still seemed like a fantasy. His mum was particularly worried as the band began taking up more and more time. Just as he'd seemed to be getting his life together and enjoying his college course, it looked like he was about to throw it all away for some band.

# 2
# ESSEX BAND

Composition of Sound had already played a couple of gigs as a three-piece, even before Dave joined – Andy on bass and Vince and Martin on synths. They were more of a curiosity than anything else. Their first gig was at school and they were soon surrounded by kids who'd never seen synthesisers before, trying to press the buttons and find out what they did. They didn't have a drummer, mostly because they didn't know anybody who had a drum-kit and, anyway, drums were far too noisy. They used to rehearse at Vince's house with headphones on but even then his mum would complain about the clacking of the keys.

When Dave joined it wasn't long until they decided to go fully electric, persuading Andy to switch from bass to synthesiser. Vince loved pure pop but the fact that they were electronic gave them a slight experimental edge. Other keyboard bands were being lumped into the so-called 'Futurist' scene. They weren't sure about that but they preferred it to the alternative, which was to be nascent New Romantics, more interested in the clothes than the music. The term 'New Romantics' had not yet been coined but already, in reaction to the ugliness of the late 1970s punk scene, there was a group of hipsters centred around clubs like Billy's in London who were developing a more androgynous, glamorous style. Later on, bands like Spandau Ballet, Duran Duran and Adam and the Ants would take New Romantic into the mainstream but, although Depeche Mode flirted with the style, they were never interested in being "cool" in that sense.

At the start of their career, Martin, Andy and Vince's Christian connections still came in handy. After Vince's mum got fed up with them at home, they used to practise in the local church. "You had to be nice and polite, and you weren't allowed to play too loud," Dave said later. Then in May 1980 they got their first gig as a four-piece at St Nicholas School, where Andy and Martin had been pupils. There was only one problem, they were also playing with The French Look and Martin was in both bands. It had already been a cause of friction and the driven Vince was pressurising him to choose. The band leader had his own problems, too.

"The main thing I remember about that night was that someone wanted to beat Vince up and one of our friends who was a good fighter had to step in for him and beat this other bloke up!" said Andy in 2009. The rest of the band were also surprised to see that the seemingly brash Dave suffered from horrendous nerves beforehand. He bought some cans of lager and stood outside repeatedly muttering: "I don't want to do it, I don't want to do it."

Yet as soon as they went onstage, the nerves disappeared. It wasn't the hardest crowd they'd play. Most of the people there, apart from the ones who wanted to beat them up, were friends. Nonetheless they were enthusiastically received. Martin even managed the changeover between bands reasonably successfully, switching clothes and images between sets.

By the time of their first proper, commercial gigs in Southend at Scamps and then the Alexandra pub, they were all feeling much more confident. The Alexandra was a biker's pub with a small club night, The Top Alex. It was better known for rock and blues but, to their surprise, they managed to win the crowd over. After that, Dave's Southend connections kicked in and they started playing more shows in the town and surrounding area.

On August 16, 1980, they got their first gig at another club that would become critical for their early success: Croc's Glamour Club in Rayleigh, near Southend. This venue and clubs like it were later dubbed 'The Blitz in the Sticks' because of their resemblance to the legendary New Romantic haunt in London's Covent Garden. At that time the phrase 'New Romantic' had yet to be widely adopted but the punters at Croc's were dressed-up, heavily made-up, and into pop music made with synthesisers. David Bowie, Roxy Music and Kraftwerk were popular, as was The Blitz founders Steve Strange and Rusty Egan's band Visage. Croc's also had another bizarre central attraction: two live alligators in a glass cage in reception.

Then on September 24, 1980, Composition Of Sound took another step upwards with a gig in the outskirts of London at the Bridge House. Over the years all kinds of different bands had played there, from the first wave of heavy metal and hard rock bands to Mod revivalists. By 1980, though, it was probably best known as a venue for so-called 'Oi' bands. 'Oi' was a punk off-shoot championed by *Sounds* journalist Gary Bushell. Its aficionados were the exact opposite of the 'Blitz Kids'. Often skinheads, they wore heavy boots and sneered at synth bands as poseurs. Not surprisingly, the first Composition Of Sound shows weren't always well attended. "When [Composition Of Sound] came along with their sort of music, we didn't know how to pigeon-hole them at the time," says Bridge House promoter Terry Murphy. "It was totally different. They were quite brave to come to a pub like the Bridge House."

Without the ready-made Southend scene to draw upon, they were lucky to get the half-dozen or so friends who'd travel up with them. Dave's girlfriend Joanne lived nearby so she persuaded a few of her friends to come along, too, but it was hardly packed out. Terry remembers that they seemed petrified the night of their first gig. The normal clientele were a mixture of skinheads, hippies and goths and in comparison the Essex boys felt extremely uncool.

"They came walking in like four office boys who've just got their first job," says Terry. "They were very shy. Dave used to be terrified. It looked like it anyway. The rest of the band had got things to do but Dave was standing there gripping the mic and staring straight ahead."

There were shouts of dissent from some of the skinheads but Terry liked them enough to give them another shot. He was getting bored of the dregs of the punk scene that were still hanging around. There was evidently a change in the air and he started wondering about signing them to his own label, Bridge House Records. It was clear, though, that there were still a few things that they needed to work on. Terry suggested to Dave that he needed to get a "prop", something to do with his hands instead of clinging self-consciously to the mic. But gradually they started to increase in confidence. "They had to work bloody hard because they weren't pulling no punters," Terry says. One early fan, though, Russell Lee, who would later DJ at Croc's, told the author that they were already something special. "My first memory of seeing them is of thinking how fantastic the songs were," he says. "How catchy they were. Bloody hell! I remember thinking, *How can this lot not make it? They've got to make it!*"

In their own way, Composition Of Sound were more punk rock and DIY than many of the careerist punk bands that were in existence by 1980. Their synths were far more portable than the traditional trappings of a rock band and they used to travel to gigs in one car or by train.

"I think without knowing it," Dave once said to *Rolling Stone*, "we started doing something completely different. We had taken these instruments because they were convenient. You could pick up a synthesiser, put it under your arm and go to a gig. You plugged directly into the PA. You didn't need to go through an amp, so you didn't need to have a van."

Vince was also writing better and better songs but the rest of them were occasionally frustrated by his wavering self-confidence. He'd play them demos that they really liked but then suddenly decide that he didn't want to record them after all. Some of those songs they even played at the Bridge House and many, such as the vaguely punky 'Television Set', with which they used to open shows, were fans' favourites ('Television Set' and other lost Depeche Mode songs including 'Reason Man', 'Let's Get Together' and 'Tomorrow's Dance' appeared on a bootleg of a Bridge House show).

Gradually Composition Of Sound were starting to build up a following, although they still found it hard to get gigs in central London. Still, at Croc's and at the Bridge House they were appreciated by steadily expanding crowds. This was reciprocated with the door money they received.

"I paid them £15 for their first show," says Terry. "Then they graduated to £20. Once they started pulling a crowd they'd get 70% of the gate. Then we started charging 30p or 40p on the door. So they'd make £60 or £80 a night."

They were notably different from most of the other bands who played at the time. While many of the punk and Mod acts were living the rock 'n' roll lifestyle, hanging around drinking until four in the morning after shows and then crashing out, Composition Of Sound's attitude was very different. "They never ever stayed around drinking," says Terry. "They never crashed out at the Bridge.

## DAVE GAHAN

A couple of them had jobs so they had to go to work the next day. A lot of other bands you'd be going, 'F***ing bands, hurry up!' after they'd played. But with [Composition Of Sound] it'd be twenty minutes, half hour maximum, gone."

Eventually their professionalism and persistence was rewarded by a gig upstairs at the famous London jazz venue, Ronnie Scott's. It would be a crucial milestone in their career – the first gig when they dropped Composition Of Sound and took the new name: Depeche Mode. The new moniker was Dave's suggestion. While at college he'd picked up a French fashion magazine with that title. It sounded cool, even if he wasn't exactly sure what it meant. It was certainly an improvement on Composition Of Sound and much better than their other suggestions for a new band name. These had included the likes of Peter Bonetti's Boots, The Lemon Peels, The Runny Smiles and The Glow Worms.

Although their career seemed to be heading upwards, Depeche Mode were still struggling to get gigs in the centre of London. This was despite them constantly heading into clubs and venues to play a three-track demo tape they'd recorded that consisted of two instrumentals and one of Vince's best songs, 'Photographic'.

'Photographic' was jittery and high-tempo, more sinister than anything else he'd come up with. This cold vibe was helped by a deadpan vocal from Dave that was much more similar to other electronic bands, such as the Human League, than his later style. Vince and Dave also began taking the demo to record companies in London but they got a similarly cold response. They'd walk into labels without an appointment and ask that they listen to the tape. Often the receptionist would politely suggest that they leave the cassette but they'd have to admit that they only had one copy. Perhaps more bizarrely, some more receptive A&R departments actually let them in to play the tape.

One day they visited twelve labels without any joy. In desperation they even visited the famous Rough Trade. It hadn't been their first choice because its indie aesthetic didn't exactly fit with Vince's pop vision. They went there with the attitude that a label who'd signed so many commercial 'flops' surely wouldn't be too high and mighty to sign them. They didn't understand that Rough Trade's anti-commercial stance was deliberate.

# DEPECHE MODE & THE SECOND COMING

In the *Do We Have To Give Up Our Day Jobs* documentary, Dave described Rough Trade as a "last resort". As it turned out, they were delighted by the response from the person they found manning the office. It was Scott Piering, later one of the most respected promoters in the music industry for his work with The Smiths, KLF and numerous others. He tapped his foot and looked genuinely impressed. Dave and Vince looked at each other, convinced that this was it. But when the tape stopped rolling, he shook his head. He said it was good but it wasn't Rough Trade's thing. Instead, he suggested, they should go with the man who'd just walked in – Daniel Miller.

Daniel Miller was a producer and musician who'd started his label, Mute Records, almost by accident. He released his own project The Normal independently and because he included an address on the record sleeve of his 1978 single, 'Warm Leatherette', he started getting sent demos. This encouraged him to put out more records, including influential electronic artist Fad Gadget and then his own imaginary band Silicon Teens. Silicon Teens was his idea of the perfect pop group, four teenagers on keyboards. In fact all the parts were played by him but it took the industry some time to get the joke. He put his records out through Rough Trade Distribution but the day he bumped into Dave and Vince he wasn't in a good mood. There were problems with Fad Gadget's record sleeve and he was trying to find out what was going on. He barely listened to the music playing. He just glanced at them briefly and probably forgot all about it. Dave, characteristically, took his non-committal response to heart. "He looked at us," he recalled later, "and said, 'Yeeuch'. We just thought, 'Bastard.'"

Their problem was that they didn't seem to fit with anything else going on at the time. The other electronic bands were mostly super-cool 'Futurists' playing keyboards as an art statement. Depeche Mode were playing keyboards because they wanted to make great pop music. They were bemused by the whole 'Futurist' scene. They found it pretentious and, as teenagers, many of the 20-something bands associated with it seemed ancient.

"I don't like that scene at all," Dave later said to early champion Betty Page of *Sounds*. "All the bands involved with it are in one bunch together and they'll never escape from it. Soft Cell are about the only ones with a good chance. I don't like to bitch, but Naked

Lunch have been going for years."

Nevertheless the band's next major step forward was a support slot with Fad Gadget at the Bridge House. Fad Gadget, whose real name was Frank Tovey, was a musician they had respect for. His music was definitely arty but it also had great wit and he was an impressive performer. "To us it was like we had finally made it," said Dave. "We were going to be sharing the stage with Fad Gadget and it was really exciting." It was also a second chance to impress Daniel Miller. He was mixing the sound for Fad Gadget so Depeche were confident that he'd see them, too. Fan Russell Lee estimates that there were roughly thirty people at the Bridge House for Fad Gadget but only perhaps ten of them had turned up in time for Depeche Mode.

"I wasn't really going to watch," Daniel Miller said to *Mojo* years later. "I was going to go out and get a burger with Frank Tovey. But this band came on, each with a mono-synth on beer crates, and Dave stood stock still with kind of a light box that he'd made shining underneath to make him look kind of gothy. I thought, *This song's really good, but it's just their first song. I'm sure they play their best song first*. But it just went on and on and on, these incredibly arranged pop songs. They were kids, and kids weren't doing electronic music at that time. It was people who'd been to art school mainly, but Depeche weren't processed by that aesthetic at all. They were doing just pop music on synthesizers. And it just worked incredibly well."

The ten or so people included scenester Stevo (who'd recently started his own label Some Bizzare), and Daniel Miller but at that point Terry Murphy was confident that he was going to be the one to sign them. "If I'd got in quick I'd have had them," he says, "but I was too busy with the record company. I had other bands. I knew I had to build them up. What's the good of putting the record out now? Nobody's going to buy it!"

But although both Mute and the Bridge House were small, independent labels, Mute did have the advantage of being home to Fad Gadget. He was much closer to their style than the music on Bridge House. Mute was a label designed for bands like Depeche Mode.

After the show, Daniel went backstage to meet them. He greeted Dave first, assuming that the frontman was probably the songwriter, but the singer, still sore at his attitude in the Rough Trade shop, pointed him brusquely in the direction of Vince, sitting quietly in a corner. "I think I told him to fuck off," Dave said later.

They were bemused to see that he looked as 'normal' as his old band name suggested. At that time it was de rigeur for members of the Futurist and New Romantic scenes to wear make-up and flamboyant clothes. Even the usually relatively conservative Fletch said later that his own stage outfit included a purple blouse altered by Vince's mum, "white football socks and bedroom slippers painted black."

Despite this they were eventually won over by Daniel's enthusiasm. It wasn't as if they had anything to lose. He didn't make them sign a contract. He just said he'd help them put a record out. "What do you want?" he asked them. "We want to be in the charts, we want to be on the radio," they said. He promised he'd do his best.

In fact he'd caught them just in time. Not long afterwards, other labels were starting to show an interest, too. With Vince's extraordinarily precocious pop talent and Dave's fresh-faced appeal, they were clearly highly marketable. They represented something that was still relatively new – electronic pop – combined with something much older, a group of four young lads who would appeal to young girls. They were taken out for dinner by various representatives of the major record labels and even offered large amounts of money up-front. It was tempting. They were broke and all still working at their day-jobs. "One of the people after us went on to sign Wham! – that whole fiasco," Martin Gore told *Uncut*. "I'm sure if we'd have signed to any one of those major labels we wouldn't be around today. We'd have been dropped by our second or third album."

Gradually the hipsters in Depeche Mode's audience were being replaced by real pop fans but at the start of 1981 they were still on the fringes of the avant-garde electronica scene. One early London gig took place at The Cabaret Futura, in Soho alongside performance artists the Event Group. Cabaret Futura's main aim was always to outrage and entertain. One of their favourite acts was called 'A Haircut, sir?' and involved tying one of their number upside down from a pole and ritualistically shaving their head. Cabaret Futura mainman Richard Strange said of them on his website: "In addition to the nucleus of these two members, the group could also feature, for example, eight electric bass players, or 22 cricketers in full kit."

It was a long way removed from what Depeche Mode were into. To their disgust, while they were playing, they noticed what appeared to be urine splashing down from the balconies above. The Event Group were pouring what they hoped was just yellow liquid down on them via hosepipes. It was a reminder that somewhere in the genealogy of 'Futurism' were extreme performance artists like Throbbing Gristle. Depeche Mode had not yet convinced everybody that they were very different.

One new fan, though, DJ Rusty Egan, was convinced that they could be something special. He, too, immediately tried to sign them, as he explained to the author: "I met Depeche Mode at that gig and thought they were new and original and brilliant and went mad and tried to sign them, make them stars," Rusty says. "So I started this bit about, 'I love you, I want you to play for me, I want you to do this, I want you to do that.'"

Rusty had been the drummer in The Rich Kids, the post-Sex Pistols band formed by Glen Matlock, but by then he was a full-blown evangelist for the new wave of electronic music. He was a highly influential DJ at The Blitz club along with Steve Strange and he also put on various other nights in unfashionable parts of London. He was against what he saw as the snobbery and pretentiousness of much of the avant-garde music scene. He had very clear ideas about what was and wasn't pop music.

"As far as I was concerned, 'The Model' by Kraftwerk was a pop record and should have been a Number 1," he says. "But I wasn't into Tangerine Dream, I was into pop music made with synthesisers by English people, not Giorgio Moroder making disco music for ailing divas."

The scene that The Blitz Kids created was fiercely elitist but it was, paradoxically, a democratic elite. Anybody could join if they were prepared to make the effort. Depeche Mode were nobody's idea of cool scenesters but the music they played was making an impression. Rusty Egan was surprised how unworldly they were. He was using to dealing with the ultra-confident New Romantics and Futurists. Depeche Mode came across as lovable kids.

## DEPECHE MODE & THE SECOND COMING

"They were the loveliest, sweetest, nicest guys you could meet," he says. "Dave was attached by a pair of handcuffs to his girlfriend (not literally). She went everywhere with him and they were in love. It was all, 'I can't answer that one, you'll have to let me talk to my girlfriend'. It wasn't like four young kids who were all up for it and ready, 'Let's go back to your flat and talk' or 'Let's go out all night', it was more like, 'No, I have to talk to my girlfriend.'"

Rusty told Dave that he could get them gigs at Flicks, his club in Dartford but it was still Croc's that was the most important venue for them. Croc's was a copy of The Blitz but, as New Romantic was essentially a suburban movement, it was by no means inferior. Boy George's Culture Club were regularly in attendance but eventually it was Depeche Mode who were the stars of their own little scene.

"It was The Blitz in the Sticks," says Rusty Egan. "Don't forget what The Blitz club was, it was unemployed, working-class people who felt that they had a talent of some sort and they had something to contribute, after no future, three million people on the dole. This was when Factory Records and Manchester and all these grey, miserable places started to produce 'industrialist' music they called it, the basis of Mute Records. At Crocs it was just the same people as at Blitz."

And, at Croc's, Depeche Mode kept running into Stevo of the Some Bizzare label. Stevo loved 'Photographic' and they were surprised to find that he saw them as a part of his scene of unusual, oddball pop. He was in the process of putting together a compilation with bands like Soft Cell and Blancmange, to be called simply *Some Bizzare*. He and Rusty shared a love of electronic music but Stevo had much more outré tastes.

"He thought he was a great DJ," says Rusty. "He would put on Cabaret Voltaire and say how brilliant that is and I'd say, 'Yeah, and it's cleared the dance floor Stevo!' You need to put on a record that people could dance to. He'd put on records by Suicide and Throbbing Gristle that would clear the dance floor."

At that point Depeche Mode's tastes were more in line with Rusty's and, when Stevo suggested they include 'Photographic' on his album, they were delighted but somewhat confused.

"We're not a bizarre band," Vince protested.

Stevo also wanted to sign them to his label for an album deal.

# DAVE GAHAN

Temptingly he could offer them a support slot with Ultravox. It could have been an awkward situation because Stevo had a club night at the Bridge House and often worked with Daniel Miller. In the end though, it was a battle that the Mute boss would win. He understood what Depeche Mode wanted, which was simply to put a record out.

Although they respected Stevo and Terry Murphy, and were confused by the major labels, it seemed much simpler to stick with Mute. Daniel's deal was just based on a handshake but they were happy with that. Later on, it would be suggested that this deal was even better than Paul McCartney's.

# 3

# SPEAK AND SPELL

The battle between Daniel Miller and Stevo to sign Depeche Mode was eventually settled when Stevo signed the other great pop hope of the Futurist scene, Soft Cell while Daniel agreed to produce both bands for the *Some Bizzare* album. Then, after re-recording 'Photographic', he took them into Blackwing Studios in south London to make what would be their first single, 'Dreaming Of Me', for Mute. Blackwing Studios was a converted church in London's Docklands, owned by Eric Radcliffe, later immortalised in the successful Yazoo album *Upstairs At Eric's*. He was one of the few studio engineers who was enthusiastic about synthesised music at the time and willing to let bands experiment.

Things were going better than they could have expected. In fact, the progress of Depeche Mode was presenting them, and Dave in particular, with a dilemma. He enjoyed his course at Southend Art College far more than he had school and he was starting to get somewhere. He'd already got the British Display Society Award, which was his ticket to a 'proper' job doing window-dressing for a big store in London. Unfortunately he hadn't finished the course and was constantly taking unauthorised days off to rehearse with the band. In the end, the headmaster had no choice but to expel him. It was a worrying moment. Nevertheless he managed to talk his way into a trainee position at the big John Lewis store on Oxford Street. All of Depeche Mode but Vince had steady jobs at this point. Martin worked in a bank and Andy had a reasonably well-paid job as an insurance clerk. In 1981 this was by no means a universal state of affairs for recent school leavers. To leave their jobs, or to potentially lose them by taking too much time off work and turning up exhausted the morning after gigs, was a big risk.

The first sign that Depeche Mode might get somewhere came when John Peel chose to play 'Photographic' on his cult radio show. It didn't mean a lot in terms of commercial success but, critically, the respected DJ carried huge clout. In February 1981, on Valentine's Day, Depeche Mode played their most prestigious gig yet, supporting Ultravox at The Rainbow in London. It was a night put on by Rusty Egan and he paid them £50 to appear along with another synth band, Metro. It was their first gig in front of a big London crowd and they made an instant impression.

The success of 'Dreaming Of Me' in 1981 helped ease their fears even further. The release enjoyed reasonable reviews although most magazines and DJs just regarded it as another cool, eccentric Mute single. Then, surprisingly, Radio One's Peter Powell – not exactly regarded as a cutting edge DJ – started playing it. At the end of March, 'Dreaming Of Me' entered the UK chart at Number 57. It didn't crack the all important Top 40 but it was Number 1 in the indie chart and would ultimately be the best-selling indie single of the year. Interestingly the excellent b-side, 'Ice Machine', sounds a lot more like later Depeche Mode than its more famous a-side. It has a much darker, more powerful sound – a trait reflected in the fact that they were still playing the song live right up until 1984. But the poppy 'Dreaming Of Me' was the beginning of the end of their reputation as cool outsiders. There was already a growing divide between the acts who would form the new, so-called 'indie' scene and pop bands like Depeche Mode.

"There was a North–South divide with the Mancunians, the raincoat brigade we called them," says Rusty Egan. "They were furious people who read Dostoevsky and Sartre. Young pop people making pop records with synthesisers was looked upon as selling out, I suppose. Then along came New Order who found a drum machine and had bigger hit records than anybody."

The divide was never as big as it was made out to be, perhaps. Martin Gore would later start reading authors like Herman Hesse, Camus, Kafka and Brecht, but the perception was that Depeche Mode were moving inexorably into the mainstream pop world. Still, they didn't care. 'Dreaming Of Me' was, very nearly, a hit and they were beginning to attract industry attention even outside of the UK.

In April 1981, high-powered American music executive Seymour Stein was in the country. He'd worked with Daniel Miller in the past and always spent time investigating the UK independent scene at the Rough Trade shop. Daniel suggested that he come and see Depeche Mode. That's how the man who signed Talking Heads, The Pretenders and later Madonna came to spend the night at Raquel's club in Basildon. After the show he wanted to come backstage to meet the band but it was so small that there was no backstage as such. Instead they chatted to him on the stairs. He was highly impressed and, although he didn't offer them anything there and then, he told them to keep in touch.

Despite their increasing success, Dave had always intended to keep his job regardless but an incident in early 1981 made him change his mind. He was working in the window of John Lewis when somebody tapped on the glass and mouthed, "Are you in Depeche Mode?" He should have been pleased but he felt faintly ridiculous and handed in his notice that afternoon.

Arguably their second single, 'New Life', recorded once again at Blackwing Studios, vindicated that decision. It was ultra clean and poppy with a chorus that was much bouncier than anything their *Some Bizzare* contemporaries had yet come up with. Sure enough it leapt out of the art-pop ghetto and on to daytime radio. It peaked at Number 11 in the charts and went on to sell over 200,000 copies. It also brought them the holy grail of all pop groups in the 1980s – an appearance on *Top Of The Pops*. Depeche Mode had 'arrived'.

The day of the famous TV show's recording didn't exactly feel the way the young band had expected it to. They hadn't been given any kind of advance by Mute so they had to travel there by train from Basildon and then by Tube across London. Martin and Andy still had their day jobs and they hardly looked like pop stars. They were wearing shirts and ties and looking every bit like clerks on their day off. When they got to the BBC studios, they even had problems trying to convince the doormen that they were supposed to be there. Nevertheless, introduced by presenter Peter Powell as "Depech-ay Mode" (as they used to insist it was pronounced), they mimed with huge enthusiasm. And there was one advantage of having a day job that Dave missed out on – when Andy walked into work the next day he was given a standing ovation by his colleagues.

As the band got bigger, even Dave's anxious mum had to admit that it seemed like he might have done the right thing. The idea of

# DAVE GAHAN

a child, left by their father, desperately searching for love through performance is something of a cliché but for Dave Gahan there might be some truth in it. Certainly as Dave got older he accepted that the desire to be acclaimed was a major driving force in his personality. He was never sure, though, if things would have been different had his dad been around. Besides, his mum always provided a stable environment for all of her children, which did just as much to shape him. After the initial success of Depeche Mode, he became curious about Len again and he asked Sylvia if she had any pictures. She produced one that showed him in a pub and Dave recognised the similarity. "Yeah, that's my old man, all right," he commented wryly.

With their appearance on *Top Of The Pops*, Depeche Mode were now considered a true success by all of their friends and family. In the 1980s it was almost as though bands didn't exist unless they went on the programme. In the band's own eyes, though, they had much further to go. That same week they went back into Blackwing Studios and then spent six weeks there with Daniel Miller producing their debut album; the result was very different to anything they would come out with later on in their career. They had the songs already. They'd been playing them for a year and a half and all they had to do was go into the studio, put the headphones on and perform them as they had done so many times before on stage.

The result was a strange mixture of avant-garde influences and pop melodies. All of the songs but two were written by Vince Clarke and he had a decidedly unusual aesthetic. He loved clean, bright sounds and had a distaste of anything overly pretentious or dark. It was highly camp and yet Dave's laddish, Essex boy vocals provided songs like 'New Life' with a distinctive counterpoint to the light melodies.

They decided to call the record *Speak And Spell*, after the hugely popular educational toy of the late 1970s and early 1980s. It was a title that neatly ties the album to the time it was made. The synthesisers they were using were only slightly more sophisticated than the toy and yet they'd managed to conjure up some extraordinary sounds out of them. Later on the band would largely dismiss *Speak And Spell* as little more than the beginning of a long learning curve and yet much of it still stands up very well today. Even the limitations of the technology give it a certain naïve charm. Admittedly there were a couple of clangers. The pseudo-camp anthems 'Boys Say Go!' and 'What's Your Name?' sounded awkward and contrived. Nobody in the band was actually gay and yet for Vince, as he proved with his later work with Erasure, a certain cheeky camp seemed to be part and parcel of pop music.

Unfortunately, in retrospect, both tracks were little more than dry runs for the work Vince would do with Erasure. However, another camp pop track, 'Just Can't Get Enough', was a different matter. It would be the one song from the first four years of their career that they would still happily play in the 1990s and beyond. When they released it as a single in September 1981, prior to the release of the album, it was the track that was to push them into the pop stratosphere, losing them their place among the cool set of *Some Bizzare* and hurtling them into a more lucrative home in the hearts and record collections of teenage girls throughout Britain.

The video also saw the classic incarnation of what Dave would later describe as their "gay leather" look. It was a style that they'd later feel they abandoned much too soon. They may have been mocked at the time but it was surely much better than the suits that they'd later sport. Throughout the first half of their career, Depeche Mode seemed to struggle to get the visual side of being in a band right and this was borne out by the artwork for *Speak And Spell*. Daniel Miller suggested they use photographer Brian Griffin. He was well known for his work with bands such as Echo And The Bunnymen and he'd helped those Liverpool legends forge a distinctive visual identity.

When Brian came to meet them he was exactly what they expected from an artist. He was wearing a big floppy hat and waving his arms excitedly. He told them he had a vision of a swan flying through the air. They were impressed but worried about how much it would cost. The result, though, didn't quite turn out as they'd expected. "It sounded really great," Brian told this author. "But it turned out to be a stuffed swan in a plastic bag! It was meant to be all nice and romantic, but it was just comical! I don't really know what I was trying to do. It was voted as one of the worst album covers of all-time! It was really slack."

# DAVE GAHAN

Prior to the release of the record, Depeche Mode had the chance to present themselves in a different way with their first *NME* cover. At the time *NME* was hugely popular, with a circulation of many hundreds of thousands. It was also known for a certain cynicism and a band like Depeche Mode, so overt about their desire to be pop stars, didn't quite fit with its post-punk ethos. This was perhaps expressed by the cover photograph, which featured Dave Gahan in front of the rest of the band. He was undoubtedly happy about this until the Wednesday morning when he received his copy of the paper and saw that his image was blurred while the rest of the band were clear and sharp. He didn't understand.

"I was really disappointed," he said later. "I was on the front but … I wasn't. It was quite cheeky of him [the photographer]. It went completely over my head, the whole photograph. I remember thinking, 'What a bastard! He's got me completely out of focus.'"

It's fair to say that the photographer wasn't all that keen on their music. He was a young, Dutch snapper who'd become famous because of his work with Joy Division. His name was Anton Corbijn and, many years later, he would become a massive part of Depeche Mode's history.

They weren't the only electronic band about go over the top in a big way that year. Human League's *Dare* was about to make them pop stars. Soft Cell's cover of 'Tainted Love' would become one of the hits of the 1980s, OMD's *Architecture And Morality* was their biggest album yet and, overseas, there were acts like Yello and Jean Michel Jarre all selling millions of records. When 'Just Can't Get Enough' was released as a single in September 1981, it made Depeche Mode household names but it also distanced them from their cooler contemporaries. This was later summed up by *Rolling Stone* critic David Fricke who said, in a review of the first batch of English synth pop albums of the early 1980s: "Compared to Soft Cell's smutty pop, Depeche Mode's *Speak And Spell* is strictly PG-rated fluff. A group of fresh-faced, suburban lads from Britain, they have neither the ambition of Orchestral Manoeuvres In The Dark nor the overt commercial allure of the Human League." However Fricke regarded the trend for synthesised pop in the UK as a "fad" and went on to declare, with spectacular inaccuracy, "If this batch of records is any indication, the revolution will not be synthesised."

# DEPECHE MODE & THE SECOND COMING

Depeche Mode had apparently lost any critical kudos they might have enjoyed in the past. They were in a very different world now; the world of Duran Duran, Spandau Ballet and the other synth acts who were no longer 'New Romantics' or 'Futurists' but simply pop bands. Despite this, they didn't turn their back on the enthusiasts who'd supported them at the start.

"They never ever showed any disdain towards me or Steve Strange," says Rusty. "Others did and went into that 'now we're rock stars' or 'now we're pop stars' thing. Depeche Mode always said thank you for all the support I gave them and all the early gigs."

Depeche Mode didn't care too much about what happened to be hip. They just wanted to write good songs. Unfortunately the man who'd been most responsible for their teen-friendly sound, Vince Clarke, was also the one who felt the most uncomfortable with their new status. He'd never enjoyed giving interviews and he was startled by what he felt were uncomfortable invasions into their privacy.

This came to a head after an interview with Rick Sky of the *Daily Star* newspaper. Rick asked if they thought it was an advantage to be good looking and Vince replied that of course it was. "Rick Sky made it out that Vince had said ugly bands never make it and if you're good looking then you're Number 1," said Dave afterwards. Vince was peculiarly affected by this relatively innocuous example of tabloid journalism. For several weeks he hardly bothered leaving his flat and from then on he left interviews to the rest of the band. They were worried about him but nobody expected him to react the way he did. At that point they were incredibly busy with promotion and performing.

Dave was still only 19, while Martin and Andy were 20 and Vince was 21. They hadn't yet found the confidence to take control of what was going on around them, or to ignore criticism. Brian, who worked with them for many years afterwards, says that he got very little impression of what they were like at those first meetings. "They were like really young boys from Basildon," he says. "They weren't unruly at all, like some other band members can be. They were quite disciplined."

With the release of 'Just Can't Get Enough', their days of playing Croc's were over. It was an exciting development but, at times, a terrifying one too. This was particularly true for Dave who was the object of most of their fans' attention. On one occasion he was asked to make a personal appearance at the Camden Palace to sign autographs and chat to the kids. A few months before it would have been easy and enjoyable but their audience had changed.

"It was really scary," he said to *Sounds* magazine afterwards. "When I got inside I was trapped and there were people clawing at me, ripping my clothes, pulling my hair – I was so frightened I ran and hid myself in the loo, I just didn't want to come out. I think that was one of my worst experiences, those kids could kill you."

Still, Depeche Mode weren't daunted. They had the kind of strong work ethic that came from having had dull day jobs. Whatever happened they were adamant that they didn't want to go back to that. Dave, in particular, having had a taste of stardom, was in no hurry to go back to being a window-dresser.

But, in November 1981, it looked like that might be exactly what was about to happen.

# 4
# DON'T GO

Dave knew that Vince wasn't happy but he didn't know how upset he was. Vince had always been something of an introvert and although they'd got on well initially, there was now a distance between them. In September 1981 they'd reached another milestone for the band – their first overseas tour. The first date was in Hamburg, just as it had been for another teenage band, The Beatles, twenty years previously. They went on to Amsterdam, then Brussels, then Paris. For almost the whole time, though, Vince just sat at the front of the van barely talking to anybody.

Ironically, one problem for Vince was the kind of attention that came along with his teen-friendly songs. He didn't like having to do all the interviews and the photo-shoots. He was happiest when writing or working in the recording studio. Equally, he didn't like the democratic nature of bands. Many years later, in an interview with *The Times* about his later vehicle, Yazoo, he admitted. "I lacked the life-skills of communication in a relationship, I felt confident in the studio, but starting a chat with somebody..."

He didn't like it when the rest of the band questioned the songs he was writing. They'd always been dubious about his lyrics, for example. For Dave, who actually had to sing them, they could occasionally be painful. He had particularly bad memories of 'New Life'.

"I remember," he recounted to Mark Ellen of *Smash Hits* in 1982, "walking through town in Basildon one night and I saw these two girls following along behind me. I knew they'd recognised me. And they start singing, y'know, 'I stand still stepping on a shady street'. And I start walking a bit faster, turns me collar up like this! And then (wails) 'And I watch that man to a stranger.' And I'm thinking: *Oh no, this is embarrassing! Do they understand these lyrics?! Perhaps they do and we don't!*"

Vince often wrote words to fit a tune, that was his common

approach. On one occasion he gave the rest of the band three new songs he'd written but when he went off to the toilet they turned to each other and said, "These are shit! We can't record these!" When he got back they told him in only slightly more polite terms. "That may have been the turning point," Martin said to *Mojo* years later.

With hindsight Terry Murphy thinks that Vince was sizing up a new direction one night at the Bridge House. "I had an idea that Vince was pulling out when he came down to see Alison Moyet," he says. "He came round to see her play with her band the Little Roosters and he said to me, 'Alison comes from Basildon and I thought I'd come down and see her.' I thought at the time that he was going to take Alison into Depeche. They're busy guys, once they make it they don't just come out to see gigs as such. I thought, *What's he doing?* It's a joke getting Alison in because she had this deep voice. I couldn't make it out."

Of course Vince had no intention of bringing Alison Moyet into Depeche Mode. A year or so later, as the duo named Yazoo, they would become one of the most successful bands in the country. At the end of the summer in 1981, Vince went round to Dave and Fletch's houses and informed them that he was leaving the band. They were stunned. They'd had three hit singles and the album was about to be released. They'd all given up their jobs at the peak of the worst recession for years and now this. Vince's explanation was simple.

"All the things that come with success had suddenly become more important than the music," he said to *New Sounds* after the split was announced. "We used to get letters from fans saying: 'I really like your songs'; then we got letters saying: 'Where do you buy your trousers from?' Where do you go from there?"

Vince promised to finish the tour that they had planned, and offered to carry on writing for them, but it was a massive blow. At that point they hadn't even signed a deal with Seymour Stein and Sire Records in America. So they put the release of *Speak And Spell* back. "To be honest it was a complete disaster as far as I was concerned," says Terry Murphy. "They'd lost the writer. That was their strength, the songs. I thought that was the end of them completely. I couldn't believe it when he left." It was hard to imagine Martin being the one to take over. They were all very shy and quiet in the band but he was probably the least imposing. Fletch often acted as 'manager' and Vince and Dave were the obvious focal points.

"Martin was the quiet one in the corner," says Terry. "Never said a word. None of them said much. You had to speak to them first and it wasn't big-headedness, it was shyness, coming to this big London town gig from Basildon."

Despite this, they never contemplated giving up. With the confidence of youth they thought that they could simply carry on with Martin as chief songwriter. "I think we should have been slightly more worried than we were," said Martin later. "When your chief songwriter leaves, you should worry a bit."

Depeche Mode carried on touring regardless, playing fourteen dates in October and November 1981, before Vince's last ever show at the Lyceum in London on November 16. At that point he could justifiably have thought that Depeche Mode was finished. Their new 'songwriter', Martin, was an extremely shy, unforceful character and neither Dave or Fletch were renowned musicians. Initially there was some animosity towards him for his sudden departure but that soon faded away.

"Maybe when Vince left there was the thought for just a moment that we should all whack him after we'd just given our jobs up and all that," said Andy to *Blitz* Magazine in 1986, "but even the split was quite amicable, we just went straight back into the studio and carried on recording."

After Vince's departure they needed to prove that they still had a future, to themselves as much as anyone else. With this in mind, before *Speak And Spell* was even released, they recorded a track, 'See You', that Martin had written when he was 17. It was inspired by the early 1960s pop that his mother had loved and it was a strange mixture of his own style and a degree of aping Vince. The version that would later appear on their second album started with a dark, sinister melody that quickly reverted to something soft and sweet. The single's mix, though, leapt as quickly as possible into the chorus. It suggested that they were more worried than they were letting on about surviving without Vince's melodies.

Nevertheless the results were good enough to make them confident that they didn't need to replace him. In the short term, though, they still needed to find somebody to play his keyboard parts on their next tour. To that end they put a very blunt advert in *Melody Maker* magazine.

"Name band, Synthesizer, Must Be Under 21", it read.

Alan Wilder said later that he guessed it might be Depeche Mode. There weren't that many 'name bands' who were under 21, who'd recently lost a member and who were so proud of their synthesisers. He was 22 at the time and had been in several different bands already, without much success. His current band, The Hitmen, wasn't going anywhere, so he went along to the audition at Blackwing Studios.

By the time he got there, Depeche Mode were starting to get disillusioned. Daniel Miller was vetting the applicants and the standard was not high. Predictably, many colourful characters turned up for the auditions but the standard of musicianship was not what they had wanted – until Alan Wilder entered the room. He could play anything. For his part, Alan was surprised at how rudimentary some of the music was. He thought many of their parts could be played with little more than a single prodding finger. He also instinctively felt that he didn't exactly fit in with Dave, Martin and Fletch. They seemed very Basildon. "All their friends were from Basildon and Alan came from a slightly different – slightly posher, in their eyes – background," Daniel Miller said to *Uncut*. "He was musically very adept and, at the beginning, slightly snobbish about the fact that everything they played was one-finger monophonic stuff."

"It was a little tricky," he said later. "I'm sort of middle-class, they were working-class lads. They were young, they seemed very naïve. Musically I thought they were a bit naïve-sounding, but there was something interesting about it, and I was sort of in a desperate situation where I would take just about any gig at the time."

And although they too might have been in an uncertain situation after the departure of Vince, Depeche Mode were a band who'd just had two Top Twenty hits and were about to release a much-anticipated debut album. It can't have been a difficult decision even if, secretly, Alan did think that the rest of the band were a bit musically unsophisticated.

The real reason that Vince left may have been simply that he thought he could do better without them. At the time it was a fair point. One of the songs that Depeche Mode dismissed as "shit" was the excellent 'Only You', which would later become a massive hit for Vince with Alison Moyet in his new band Yazoo. The first two Yazoo singles, 'Only You' and the brilliant 'Don't Go' – both of which went Top Three – made it strikingly obvious who was the more accomplished songwriter at that time. In an interview with *The Times* in 2008, Alison Moyet said that there was "an awareness [between her and Vince] that 'Only You' was far superior to 'See You.'"

For all their denials, at the time this awareness was partly shared by Depeche Mode. They couldn't help but be envious, as Vince seemed to go from strength to strength. "I think we were kind of jealous, to be honest," Dave admitted years later in an interview with *Rolling Stone*. "The first song that they had out, 'Only You,' was a song he tried to give us. And I was like, 'I don't think so.' And, of course, then it was a huge hit."

For Mute, it ultimately turned out to be a win-win situation. Daniel Miller now had two name bands. Vince's Yazoo were enormously successful and his departure from Depeche Mode presented an opportunity for Martin. Still, there was occasionally slight friction when they'd bump into each other in the Mute office. They didn't feel able to complain too much, though. They all knew Alison Moyet from school in Basildon and she'd been regarded with trepidation.

"She was in our class at school and she was the best fighter in the year!" Fletch said to *Uncut*. "Once, when we were in this small Mute office, she thought we were laughing at her and she said, 'Fletch, if you laugh at me once again I'll kick you in the bollocks.' Never laugh at Alison Moyet."

When *Speak And Spell* finally came out, it went Top Ten but the obituaries for Depeche Mode were already being written. The two songs Martin had written on their debut album, 'Tora Tora Tora' and the instrumental 'Big Muff' were pretty good but there was no sign yet that he could write hits like Vince Clarke. It was noticeable, though, that 'Tora Tora Tora' had a darker, dirtier sound than anything Vince had come up with. In retrospect it's much closer to the kind of music for which they'd become revered.

For now though Alan was joining a band who were the epitome of a lightweight pop act. Their videos were generally made in the bright, primary colours of children's TV and their photo-shoots were often frankly embarrassing. It was, however, a formula that remained successful.

'See You' was released at the start of 1982 and, to their relief, it went Top Ten. Bizarrely it did better than their far superior previous single 'Just Can't Get Enough', a testament to the loyalty of their teen fanbase. The success of 'See You' was a major boost. It proved that the three of them could make a go of it on their own. It also made them think, in retrospect unwisely, that they didn't need the assistance of another keyboard player in the studio. Alan was there simply to play on stage. They paid him a weekly sum initially and he made his debut at Croc's in January 1982. There wasn't time to think about what they were doing or where they were going. Immediately after the Croc's show they headed off to New York for their first gigs in America.

It should have been a great opportunity. 1982 was the beginning of the so-called Second British Invasion. Since the advent of *MTV* British bands – generally more image conscious than their American counterparts – had made a major splash in the States. Acts like Duran Duran, Culture Club, Wham! and ABC would soon become huge stars. At the peak of the Second British Invasion in July 1983, eighteen of the Top 40 singles on the *Billboard* Chart in America were British.

But Depeche Mode's shows didn't go well. Mute decided to fly them over for their first gig, at the Ritz Club in New York, by Concorde. Unfortunately, after that bright start, things went rapidly downhill. Dave, by now, was regretting one aspect of his teenage wildness. He was very settled with his childhood sweetheart Joanne and, just before leaving, he had the worst of his old tattoos removed. This caused severe scarring that swelled up so badly he had to perform with his arm in a sling. When they got on stage they had constant technical problems and faced a sea of disappointed faces. It was like a confirmation of the stereotypical American rock fan's view that synth music wasn't "real" music at all.

This might not have been such a problem but their early videos were notoriously awful. The strangest, perhaps, was 'See You'.

# DEPECHE MODE & THE SECOND COMING

They hired Julien Temple as the director, then best known for his film about The Sex Pistols, *The Great Rock And Roll Swindle*. He went on to make acclaimed documentaries on Joe Strummer and Glastonbury, among many fine films. He was by no means the typical pop director but his Depeche Mode videos for 'See You' and other singles were later perceived as a source of some embarrassment to the band.

The problem, perhaps, was that he directed them as though he was making miniature feature films. This would have been fine but they weren't actors and so to many observers the results were rather cringe-worthy. In 'See You', for example, Dave goes into a photo booth and gazes wistfully at a selection of photos of his missing beloved, looking like he wished he could be anywhere else but there.

"We hated making videos right from the start," said Martin in 1993. "We never felt we could trust the directors. You're totally in the director's hands. You've no idea how it's looking when you're filming it. You don't see it until it's finished and by then it's too late to change anything. It's got to go out."

Depeche Mode constantly played live throughout the first couple of years. This included a triumphant return to the Bridge House in Canning Town. It was very different to the days when they'd struggled to bring along a handful of people. Although officially a "secret" gig, there were already hundreds of fans arriving as soon as the pub doors opened at lunchtime. "It was unbelievable the number of people there at one o'clock in the afternoon," says Terry Murphy. "I had to sling them out so I could get them to pay to come back in later. It was bedlam."

The difference in their stage presence in just six months was palpable. They had a whole new confidence. Playing to hundreds of people in a venue where they'd once struggled to bring twenty vividly illustrated how far they'd come. Terry Murphy was ecstatic when he came backstage to give them the money from the door. The pub had been struggling and it looked like it was about to close.

"There was a grand or two grand there," he says. "It was well over a thousand pounds and they said, 'No, no, you keep it. Keep the pub open. It was a great gig!' It was very nice of them because they weren't rich at all, they were still penniless!"

Part of the change in the band came from the new confidence Alan's musical skill had given them. In later years, his exceptional ability in the studio would also prove to be a huge boost for the band, not least when so much of their material was electronic-based. Despite this, Alan wouldn't yet become a full member of the band for almost two years – a route that many founder members of bands take when they initially welcome in a new face to their inner circle. To begin with Alan received a modest wage, said to be somewhere between £100 and £200 a week. Again this was not uncommon.

The shows in mainland Europe were a particularly bizarre initiation. Despite the fact that pioneers Kraftwerk came from Germany, Depeche Mode were seen almost as a kind of freakshow in much of the Continent. The press had read about England's New Romantic scene and Depeche Mode were constantly asked if they were "Blitz Kids". Often journalists and TV presenters seemed a little bemused by these naïve kids from Basildon. On one early performance for Swedish TV, Dave was asked what their lyrics meant and he had to admit that they had no idea.

"I don't know," he told the confused interviewer. "Vince recently left the band. We always asked him what the lyrics meant but we still don't know."

This would have been a reasonable thing to say except that the song they were about to perform, 'See You', was written by Martin! They were also starting to create a stir in mainland Europe where the English synth bands were considered by the mainstream as something of a curiosity.

"Do you think synthesisers can replace real instruments totally?" Dave was asked and it's interesting that, rather than pointing out that synthesisers are real instruments, he politely said, "No, I think there'll always be guitars and drums." On another TV appearance in Holland, the curious presenter went round the band asking, "And who's the guitarist? And the bass player? The drummer?" They were then forced to explain that they didn't actually have any of those people before Dave gave them a guided tour of the keyboards and "the drummer", a squat-looking tape machine. At this point they

## DEPECHE MODE & THE SECOND COMING

also gave up insisting that people pronounce their name Depech-ay. Initially they'd liked the way it sounded French and sophisticated, when in fact the French pronunciation was more like "Depesh".

For his part Alan agreed to take part in all the promotional work that they were asked to do. This was undoubtedly the lowest point of Depeche Mode's entire career in music and fashion terms. They didn't look great and they accepted most tasks they were asked to do without demur. These included some pretty astonishing TV performances. On a German show called *Bananas* they were filmed miming to 'See You' in a barn filled with straw. Initially Dave just looks faintly silly, wearing a terrible suit and high-waisted trousers. Then the cameraman cuts to footage of him sitting down holding a chicken, as other fowl wander among their feet. The look on Alan's face as he grimly clutches his chicken is priceless. As if that wasn't enough, behind them, rather contradicting the song's prim message, a couple roll about in the hay.

It wasn't just overseas that they were forced into some embarrassing situations either. Dave and Martin appeared on Saturday Morning TV show *Tiswas* attempting to answer the usual questions ("Why do you use synths?" "Why are you called Depeche Mode?" "How do you pronounce Depeche Mode?") while rowdy kids sat directly behind them, chatting and laughing among themselves. The children only appeared to pay attention at the end when they were given the order to throw bits of paper over the two stars and plant a cream pie in Dave's face.

Even more embarrassingly, around the same time, they also appeared on British 1980s institution *Jim'll Fix It*. It was a long-running programme in which children wrote in to the presenter, the decidedly eccentric Jim Saville, asking him to "fix it" for them to achieve some dream that they had. One girl's dream was to perform with Depeche Mode so they duly went on and let her play keyboards before Alan presented her with a trophy, the treasured *Jim'll Fix It* badge.

At the time there was a major divide between 'pop music', which was considered by many TV and radio programmers as simply entertainment for children and 'rock music', which was for teenagers. Anybody over 30 who still liked either was considered somewhat bizarre. Depeche Mode had no qualms about children

## DAVE GAHAN

buying their records but they were slowly realising that their image could potentially mean that teenagers and adults wouldn't.

# 5

# A BROKEN FRAME

When Depeche Mode went into the studio to record their second album, *A Broken Frame*, they may have been painfully conscious of the distance between Yazoo's brilliant singles leaping up the charts and the rather listless songs that they had composed without Vince. At least they had an excuse. Martin Gore had been forced into the position of having to write a whole album in a matter of weeks.

"We were floundering around not knowing where to go," said Martin to *Kingsize* magazine in 2001. "It was the first time I'd taken over the songwriting, and it was a real mishmash. Some tracks were old, among the first things I'd written, and others I came up with on the spot."

They recorded at Blackwing Studios again but this time it wasn't such a fun experience. "It's a really strange place,' Dave said to *Record Mirror* at the time. "There's a statue of Christ on the cross that someone's painted with blood outside in the garden. We had a load of photos down there, but none of those came out. It's really weird."

They were all still living in Basildon and so they'd get the train to London Bridge every morning and then get the last train back at night. By now, of course, their faces had appeared in all the pop magazines and they'd been on TV numerous times so they were often recognised and not always in a good way. Many of the people on the train were 'Essex geezers' who'd been drinking since finishing their day's work in London. "We always got into fights," said Martin, "sometimes because we were recognised, but usually it was just pure Essex violence!"

Dave complained later that, "people were letting us drift". He said that for the second album there was a lack of enthusiasm in the studio. They knew that they didn't want to be seen as kiddy-pop idols anymore but they weren't sure what they would replace Vince's sound with. They had a vague idea that they wanted to be "darker" than they had been and yet songs like 'See You' were almost sickly sweet. Martin's task was made harder by the fact that he was still living under the shadow of Vince. Initially he admits that he was (perhaps inevitably) heavily influenced by their former band-mate's style. They knew there was a risk that if they departed too far from what had made them successful then nobody would be interested anymore.

Depeche Mode wanted to prove that they could survive as a three-piece without Vince; as yet, the productive partnership with Alan Wilder was untapped. They desperately wanted to sound more serious and adult but the attempt wasn't entirely successful. In reality, rather than being "deeper", the songs were perhaps just more pretentious than those on *Speak And Spell*.

Perhaps the album's greatest weakness is that Martin hadn't yet started to write songs that made the best of Dave's voice. They were mostly soft, slow affairs that he could easily have sung himself. In many of the better tracks, 'Monument', 'My Secret Garden' and 'Satellite', Dave's uncharacteristically restrained. The whole record is very minimalist and 2-D. When it veers away from this, with the faster, more expansive 'Photographs Of You' it's again like somebody trying to play a 1950s pop song on a child's toy.

Later the album would be remembered more for its cover image than for the music. Despite their feelings about the artwork for *Speak And Spell,* they once again gave Brian Griffin the job of taking the picture. "It was marvellous of them that they stuck by me," says Brian, "because the next one was one of the most famous album covers of all-time." The cover of *A Broken Frame* was later used on the cover of a *Life Magazine* feature about colour photography in the 20$^{th}$ Century. This time, after the fiasco of *Speak And Spell's* swan, the band took a closer interest in what Brian was doing. "We had meetings and meetings about it, with Daniel and the band," Brian says, "and we came up with the idea that we were going to do a peasant in a corn field."

Despite this, the cover was shot in the spontaneous fashion that was Mute's hallmark. Brian's stylist Jacqui Frye was given the task of making a peasant's costume on the Friday for a shoot on Monday. Then, when they got to the cornfield near Saffron Walden in north Essex, an impatient farmer asked them to hurry up because he wanted to mow it. For most of the day it rained constantly but when the clouds cleared, Brian skillfully got a perfect image of brooding clouds and glowing corn.

"I was very fortunate when the clouds broke in such a wonderful way and I got this piece of magic," says Brian. "When I saw the Polaroid it freaked me out. I couldn't believe it. We invited Daniel Miller back to my studio to see what I'd done and we all sat in the corner waiting for him going, 'Go on Daniel, go and look in the lightbox, have a look.'"

It is technically a great picture. It was almost Social Realist in its fetishisation of labour (and that was a direction they'd go even further along with the artwork for their next album). For now, though, *A Broken Frame* had done its job. Although far from a classic, it had shown that Depeche Mode weren't finished as a creative force. "I don't think the second album was a masterpiece," admitted Martin years later. "We just got about got away with it."

"I think we all feel that *A Broken Frame* is, in retrospect, our weakest album. Definitely. It's very, very patchy," Dave said to *Melody Maker* in 1990. "That's when we got labelled as being a very doomy band. We were learning at that point. It was very naïve. It was Martin's first album as a songwriter. He was thrown in at the deep end to be honest."

At the time, they managed to half-heartedly promote it by claiming that it represented them maturing. "Whereas the stuff on the last album was Euro macho dance music, beat-y synthesizer music, this album's a lot weightier. It's got a lot more in it," Dave said.

The second Depeche Mode album was released in September 1982, just a year after their debut, to a generally positive reception and it ultimately got to Number 8 in the charts. The singles 'The Meaning Of Love' and 'Leave In Silence' also did reasonably well, reaching 12 and 18 respectively but they didn't hang around for long in the charts. Immediately afterwards, the band sensed that interest was dying away. They knew in their hearts that *A Broken Frame* wasn't a great album. They were starting to get a reputation as "wimps with synths." In Dave's case this was very far from the truth but they didn't help their cause with some of their photo-shoots and promotional appearances. On one occasion they were photographed in full cricket whites for *Smash Hits*, a picture that later came to symbolise for them their foolish willingness to do almost whatever promo they were asked to.

"We were so naïve when we came into it, but by the time of *A Broken Frame* we were beginning to realise how much of the music business was just one big farce," Dave told *NME*. "We discovered all the corruption, the big business, the marketing campaigns."

Typically they dealt with it by going back to work. For a band who've often joked about their "laziness" (the famously hard-working Alan Wilder excepted) they had an astonishing work ethic in their early years. They might have grumbled about the videos and the photo-shoots afterwards but at the time they were a PR man's dream. The music was their domain but everything else was left to outsiders. In areas like video shoots, they simply didn't have the confidence to say that they weren't happy.

The first single to be released after *A Broken Frame*, 'The Meaning Of Love', was the first video that Alan appeared in. It must have been another interesting or alarming insight into the strange world of Depeche Mode. Julien Temple had decided to take the song's search for "the meaning of love" literally so he portrayed Dave as a scientist. This meant that the video opens with a scene of him reading a book and, to demonstrate his boffin credentials even more emphatically, he's wearing glasses. Just in case this puts the kids off, there's also a bizarre, unexplained children's toys theme.

The next single, 'Leave In Silence' had an even more incongruous video. It's a slow, sombre track, one of the songs that started to change Depeche Mode's reputation from kiddy pop stars to gloom-mongers. Weirdly, though, Julien Temple seemed to take his inspiration from children's TV and *The Generation Game*. It features a conveyor belt of brightly coloured objects that the very serious-looking band hit with wooden spoons. They then started throwing balls around before chasing each other on space-hoppers. This may have captured their characters quite well. This was a band who still occasionally played 'tag' before shows until well into their recording career. But it wasn't quite the change of tone they needed.

If the seriousness on their second album had bordered on the pretentious, though, they were growing up fast. They were on the road almost constantly and during a brief gap at the end of 1982 they went back into the studio to make another single, 'Get The Balance Right'. It wasn't something they were desperate to do but

Sire, their American record label, told them that they needed a dance hit if they were going to get anywhere in the States.

The result was the most difficult experience they'd had in the studio to date. The new technology that was now available offered many advantages but it also meant there were many more things that could go wrong. For Dave, particularly, it was difficult. He wasn't a studio boffin and so he had to spend much of his time hanging around while Martin, Alan and Daniel Miller twisted the knobs.

They regarded the result as something of a disappointment but the track did, indeed, have the most powerful, modern-sounding beat of anything they'd done so far. It was only later that they found out that the 12" of the single had found its way into the clubs of Detroit, helping to inspire artists like Derrick May, who would eventually be one of the godfathers of Techno music.

"I don't know what people like about it," Dave said later. "It never really did it for us." That's understandable. As a song, 'Get The Balance Right' wasn't all that inspired. It had a somewhat weak melody and there wasn't anything in the lightweight vocal part for Dave to get his teeth into. But, although they may not have liked it, their studio experimentation on 'Get The Balance Right' pointed the way forward. Their relative success with their first two albums meant that they'd been able to afford to use the hugely expensive, state-of-the-art synthesiser the Synclavier. Also known as a "tapeless studio", because it could be used to program an entire song, it had a large range of pre-programmed sounds. More importantly for Depeche Mode's development, though, it enabled them to sample other sounds and manipulate them.

This meant, among other things, that they had to accept that Alan Wilder was more than just a session and tour musician. He was far keener on spending time in the studio than the rest of them. Dave began to feel increasingly uncomfortable about the risible weekly wage they were paying him, considering his increasing importance to the band. "I'm sure I put some pressure on, 'Either let me join or I'll go somewhere else,'" Alan has said. "I don't want to be a part-time session musician, really." After the release of 'Get The Balance Right', then, before going back into the studio, they officially announced that Alan was now a full-time member of the band.

# DAVE GAHAN

Then at the start of 1983, Depeche Mode went out to the Far East for the first time. This was to be another major influence on the next album. On a trip to Thailand they were shocked by the poverty they saw, the prostitutes on the streets and by the greed and the corruption of Western businessmen.

"You go over there and all the hotels are full of, like, businessmen and basically they tend to treat people as though they're nothing," Martin told *NME*. "All they're interested in is their business – that's what I really hate about big business, people just don't seem to matter. Just money."

It would be the first album they would make as the new Depeche Mode and there were major changes on the way.

# 6

# RECONSTRUCTION

In the spring of 1983 Depeche Mode went into electronic artist and former Ultravox singer John Foxx's Garden Studios in Shoreditch, London. Years later Shoreditch would become a magnet for artists, musicians and designers but at the time it was an area full of derelict buildings and rough pubs. There were also numerous building sites, as the area was slowly being regenerated, and these proved perfect places for the band to find sounds to sample. They took the clattering of metal, the gurgle of running water or wood being hammered against a fence and fed it all into the Synclavier. It was the kind of experimentation they could all be enthusiastic about. Even Dave and Fletch, who usually had very little input in programming the technology, were able to take part, hitting cars and throwing bricks at walls. Suddenly the enthusiasm they'd lost with the last album had returned. They'd spend days just hanging out at building sites. Their approach, though, was very different from the industrial, avant-garde bands that were around at the time. They still wanted to make pop music. They still weren't interested in a song unless it had a hook and a melody.

Significantly they started working with engineer Gareth Jones. He was known for his expertise with sampling and was to play a major part in their music over the next few years. Daniel Miller said later that his work with Depeche Mode and Gareth was among the most exciting times he'd ever had in the studio. He'd always loved experimental music but was fascinated by the way Depeche Mode were able to take it and turn it into classic pop.

The desire to get serious could have been a disaster. Innumerable pop bands have vanished largely because they decided that they were serious 'artists' rather than 'pop stars'. Depeche Mode, though, however experimental or serious they might get, have always been concerned with writing great tunes. In retrospect, they regarded *Construction Time Again* as a stepping-stone towards better things.

# DAVE GAHAN

"Some of it was very forced," Dave told Jon Wilde of *Melody Maker*. "It was a massive changing-point for us, both musically and lyrically. Maybe we were trying too hard to do too much. Sampling too much and trying to give a message without thinking so much of the structure and the point of the song."

This was undoubtedly true. Tracks like 'Two Minute Warning', 'Shame', and Alan's eco-pop 'The Landscape Is Changing' tried rather too hard to shed their pop image and provide them with a new serious persona. Furthermore the sampling wasn't as subtle or effective as it would be later. On 'Pipeline' the heavy thuds and clumps sound a little too much like the product of a building site, rather than a pop group. Still, they were the first band to try and take so-called 'industrial' music and turn it into accessible, melodic pop; there was bound to be some experimentation along the way. One of the chief differences with this period of Depeche Mode and the later phase, though, was simply how much more confident and assured Dave's voice became on later albums. It's not hard to imagine that by 2009 he could do a lot more with the fizzy, energetic 'More Than A Party' for example.

And, although it might have been flawed, *Construction Time Again* saw the beginning of a significant part of the band's history when they went to the famous Hansa Ton studios in Berlin to mix the record. They'd been recommended to go there by engineer Gareth Jones. It was where David Bowie had recorded *Heroes* in the late 1970s and, although they chose it initially because the strength of the pound made it cheap, it was an inspirational setting. Martin was particularly enthused. He'd always been fascinated by Germany, ever since a school trip there. He loved the atmosphere and the freedom of being away from English suburbia. The whole band were changing dramatically and the first product of the sessions thoroughly endorsed their new working methods, their first great single since Vince left, 'Everything Counts'.

'Everything Counts', Dave said, was a calculated effort to create something with more substance than their previous recordings. They tried to emphasise this with the video, bringing back Clive Richardson, who'd directed 'Just Can't Get Enough'. His video for 'Everything Counts' served as a kind of introduction to their new life in Berlin, the camera zooming through the city and skimming along the wall. The single reached Number 6.

The song was primarily a sign of Martin's increasing confidence. He was writing about things he'd seen in Thailand and those feelings of disgust at the lack of compassion in the business world. It would be the first single in which he would share vocal duties with Dave, providing the sorrowful chorus, while the frontman delivered the more aggressive, confident verses.

It was a great way to shake off the torpor of *A Broken Frame* but they weren't prepared for the reception that *Construction Time Again* would get. For a brief period following its release in August 1983, it seemed like they'd been rather too successful in forging a new image for themselves. This was partly because of another excellent Brian Griffin cover picture that dealt in more Soviet-style, heroic-worker imagery. It featured a man with a giant sledgehammer standing in front of the glorious panorama of the Matterhorn in the Swiss Alps.

"We took a guy who was the brother of my assistant, who'd just come out of the Royal Marines, to the Swiss Alps," says Brian, "and we took a real sledge hammer and took him up, high in the mountains, overlooking the Matterhorn."

The band just saw it as a cool photograph. They were still pretty naïve, however much they might have wanted people to believe that they were now serious artists. Despite being on their third album, Dave Gahan was still only 21. This came across in a notorious interview they did with *NME* prior to the album's release. X Moore, the lead singer of left-wing band The Redskins who wrote for the magazine at that time, saw the artwork and interviewed them in the spirit of welcoming them to an international socialist collective; he found, predictably, that they had little idea what he was talking about. In the past Fletch had characterised them as stereotypical *Sun*-reading Essex boys and, while that was obviously a cheeky over-simplification, they were far from revolutionaries.

Nevertheless the tag dogged them for a while. On one Belgian pop show they were asked to play in front of a backdrop of giant red flags and actors dressed as peasants waving hammers and sickles. "We said, 'We can't do that.' They just go, 'Oh it's OK, it doesn't have the same meaning over here,'" Dave said to *NME*'s Don Watson in

1984. "You've got twenty-foot long red flags behind you and all these heroic peasants and they expect you to believe it doesn't have any meaning. Unbelievable."

Despite the success of 'Everything Counts', when they came to choose the second single from *Construction Time Again*, there were serious divisions in the band. Quite simply there wasn't another song on the record that was anything like as good. Martin wanted 'Love, In Itself' but Dave wasn't keen at all. "This is the s-s-s-s's track," he said to *Number One* magazine. "It had a very soft vocal with lots of s's, it sounded awful. I was a bit disappointed with this, it could have been brilliant." The track does start brilliantly but it loses its way halfway through. And, as Dave said, the vocal was so soft that it sounded like he was lisping. It peaked at Number 21 in the charts, showing that their hardcore fans were still interested, then quickly fell away.

Around this time Dave decided to go for vocal lessons with renowned voice coach Tona De Brett who'd worked with everybody from John Lydon to Adam Ant. It wasn't that he'd lost confidence in his own ability but more that he wanted to improve his breathing and control, so he could run around the stage and still belt the songs out. He had an enormous touring schedule ahead of him that would last from September 1983, when 'Love, In Itself' came out through most of 1984, with only one long break to record the next album. Unfortunately he'd never been happy in 'lessons' and he didn't enjoy being taught to sing "properly".

Martin was coming out of his shell and the dynamic in Depeche Mode was changing. It must have been somewhat disconcerting for Dave. It wasn't just that his band-mate was starting to take more of an interest in books and new music. He was also going out a lot more than he had in the past. On occasion now, he was the one who'd be the centre of attention.

It seemed like Dave and Martin were going in opposite directions with Dave, at this time, craving some kind of security. He found himself missing Joanne every time he was away from her. On the rare occasions when he was back home, he liked to go fishing. He wasn't entirely domesticated, he enjoyed spending the money that had started to come in but he definitely felt like his hell-raising years were behind him.

# DEPECHE MODE & THE SECOND COMING

More importantly for the future of Depeche Mode, though, Martin was becoming increasingly interested in the new bands that he'd discovered while in Germany. In January 1984, he went to see the industrial group Einsturzende Neubauten's legendary 'Concerto For Voice And Machinery' at the Institute of Contemporary Art in London. They'd set up a cement mixer on stage and appeared with drills and chainsaws. When the authorities pulled the plug, the audience kept the noise going by smashing the place apart. It was a long way from the kind of thing Depeche Mode had been known for but Martin was inspired. In the UK, German music was still largely associated with mullets, bad rock bands and Nena's 1983 hit '99 Red Balloons', but there was an underground scene that seemed far cooler.

In 1984 Martin started going further and further with his experimentations in fashion 'cross-dressing' and make-up. He started by wearing a leather miniskirt over the top of his trousers but pretty soon the trousers had disappeared. Dave wondered what the fans would make of it. New Romantic was long since over. To begin with, though, he looked on him indulgently.

"Personally, I think he's just doing all the things I did when I was 16," he told *NME*'s Danny Kelly in 1985. "All that stuff about boredom is exactly the attitude that I went through. I went to clubs with people much older than myself. I wore tons of make-up, and dresses too. But now if I go to a club I just want to have a good time, not to shock. Nothing shocks any more. Shocking is over, unless you cut your head off or something."

Dave was very happy with his girlfriend Joanne and, although he still drank on occasion, he lived a less rock 'n' roll lifestyle than he had in his teens, before he ever joined Depeche Mode. He'd even started exercising more often to cope with the long tours Depeche Mode were now taking. He'd been alarmed at his own lack of fitness when they first headed out on the road. After one German gig he was so exhausted that when they came off stage he had to be carried to the dressing room by roadies.

"I never did any sports when I was young," he admitted to a Belgian pop magazine in 1984. "When Depeche Mode started to become a little more popular, I collapsed immediately after the first few gigs. Now I can handle it, lucky for me. Whenever I have a day

# DAVE GAHAN

off, you can find me in the gymnasium. There I train myself to exhaustion. Shadow-boxing, weight-lifting. After my German adventure I realised how difficult the life of a rock group can be."

*Construction Time Again* had just been the start. Next time, they all thought, they'd do things properly.

# 7

# REWARD

In January 1984, Depeche Mode returned to Berlin. It was soon to be a home-from-home for all of them and, eventually, Martin would move there permanently to be with his new German girlfriend. He was increasingly interested in the visual aesthetic of Berlin's seamier side, especially the imagery of the clubs and S&M scene. Apart from anything else it was a way of putting their image as cute pop kids firmly behind them.

Things were changing. By this point, partly thanks to Depeche Mode's success, Mute had become a much bigger operation and Daniel Miller was finding it difficult to give them the time they needed. In Berlin there were new tensions but also new opportunities.

At the start of the latest recording sessions, those tensions bubbled over and the band almost came to blows in the studio. Fletch and Martin were play-fighting, practising martial arts moves on each other, near Daniel's expensive equipment. When he saw them he was furious and there was, as Fletch put it, some "argy-bargy".

Ironically this occurred during the recording sessions for their next single, a song pleading for more love and understanding, 'People Are People'. It was a song that they would later repudiate, embarrassed by its simplistic lyrics yet with its clanking percussion and the earnest interplay between the voices of Dave and Martin, it was their best tune yet. Even the lyric doesn't really bring it down. On paper the infamous rhyming couplets might look pretty dreadful but Dave had a remarkable ability to sing the most clunking lines with such conviction that it didn't seem to matter.

It helped that Dave understood Martin's sense of humour in a way that maybe not everybody did. "Some of the lyrics are funny and I often chuckle to myself as I'm singing them," he said in one radio interview. They'd been sharing the same jokes since 1980 and even before that there was the Basildon background to fall back on.

## DAVE GAHAN

However, in the band, the love and understanding that they pleaded for with 'People Are People' was sometimes in short supply. Surprisingly, despite arguing frequently, Dave and Fletch never fought. Perhaps they realised that with their headstrong personalities things could get a little too serious. While Martin and Fletch were long-time best friends, Dave was slightly on the outside and Alan was even further outside him. At least by now their roles in the band were clearly defined. They still didn't have a manager as such so Fletch dealt with much of the day-to-day stuff, Martin came up with the songs and Alan was starting to put in more and more of what they called the "screwdriver work" in the studio. Dave's role was, simply, to sing, although he was always ready to offer ideas and the kind of heartfelt enthusiasm that was sometimes in short supply if tensions were present within the rest of the band. He was the only one who seemed to deeply respect Alan's increasing importance and the keyboard player appreciated that.

The band were starting to take greater control of their destiny as a whole and this included things like videos. For 'People Are People' Martin had the idea that it should reflect the 'war is bad' vibe of the lyrics and so they filmed it, with director Clive Richardson, onboard the HMS Belfast, a warship that had been turned into a museum and anchored in the heart of London. It was a good idea in theory, incorporating the metal-bashing that now helped form their sound, but in practise it still looked slightly ridiculous.

Nevertheless when 'People Are People' was released in March 1984, it went to Number 1 in Germany, making them huge stars there. In the UK it hit Number 4. It was also used in TV coverage of that year's Olympic Games where, in the time of division between East and West, the simplicity of the message was appreciated. There was something about Germany that suited Depeche Mode and the feeling was reciprocated.

Although they might have stopped playing 'People Are People' after 1988, Depeche Mode would look back on the period when they recorded it as one of the most rewarding of their career. It was a time when they were rapidly expanding what they were capable of. "We all look upon that period of recording as one of the most exciting," Alan said to *Number 1*. "We'd gone to Berlin and the feeling in the studio was very dynamic. We were aware that the single was quite close to being a disco single and we didn't want it to be like all the millions of others that were out. We wanted it to have this hard metallic sound while keeping it fairly soulful."

Living in Berlin there was always the strange consciousness of being in a kind of Western bubble. Recording in Hansa by the Wall, they were literally next door to the authoritarian socialism of East Berlin and yet it could have been hundreds of miles away. One day Martin did attempt to visit but he was turned back by the border police because of the way he dressed.

Not just Martin but the whole band ended up spending a lot of time in the city. Vince's main complaint when he left had been that there wasn't enough time to work on the music. There were too many distractions. Although they might not have felt so strongly at the time, they were all starting to feel the same way and, in Berlin, many of those distractions were eliminated. The popular impression was that they were there because of the wild nightlife but in reality it was more about the studio and about making music without England's cultural baggage.

"People imagine we work here because it's wow, you know, really heavy," said Dave, "but I don't feel that. The place is quite suburban. Berlin's like Brixton." He also added in another interview, "I can't work in England anymore."

As a result, they found themselves far removed from the British music scene. It was perhaps just as well. The halcyon days of the Second British Invasion were over and early contemporaries like Duran Duran were already starting to seem like dinosaurs. In Berlin much darker flavours were in fashion. It encouraged Martin to go ever further with his image and Dave and the rest of the band were simultaneously amused and appalled. They used to plead with him not to go out on stage dressed like that. Dave had often worn make-up as a New Romantic in the early 1980s in Basildon but he regarded it as a phase he'd grown out of. When he was asked if he'd go down the same route his answer was emphatic.

"You must be f***ing joking mate!" he said. "You won't catch me in a f***ing dress. No sodding way! I'm the yob next door. Never worn a dress in me life. Never f***ing will!" Now he found that people were laughing at him in the streets of Basildon because of something Martin was doing in the more risqué environment of

Berlin. "I certainly got a lot of stick in Basildon, that's for sure," he said, when Martin had returned to a less flamboyant style. "Thank God it's over!"

Once again he had the disconcerting feeling of being the "sensible one" compared with his more flamboyant band-mate. It must have been very odd, thinking back to the studious Martin Gore he remembered from five years' previously.

"He thought it was funny," Dave said to *Melody Maker* later. "Away from the cameras, he would be having a good old laugh about it. We'd all have a good laugh. Then we realised that it was doing none of us any good. So we kept saying to him, 'Look, you can't go out dressed like that!' Sure we did. Martin, of course, carried on doing it. These ludicrous f***ing dresses! Now he looks back and says, 'What the hell was I doing?' The funny thing was that we just about got away with it."

On the surface he may have been indulgent and a little patronising about his band-mate's fashion but, inwardly, perhaps, he felt like Martin had usurped his rightful place as the band's wildest member.

It was hard to argue with the results of Martin's new open-mindedness, though. The demos he came up with for *Some Great Reward* were much better than the previous album and, with Alan Wilder now fully integrated into the band, the sessions were among the most fulfilling they'd ever had. Dave's voice had also improved beyond all recognition.

The atmosphere at Hansa also contributed to the kind of music they were now making. Its position right next to the Wall gave it a mysterious, eerie vibe. The main hall was vast with booming, echoey acoustics and there were rumours from staff that it was haunted. This, along with the subject matter of the songs, gave the sessions an atmosphere that veered from dark Germanic seriousness to occasional outbreaks of hilarity. On one new track, 'Master And Servant', for example, they attempted to sample a whip but found it impossible. Instead they persuaded Daniel Miller to make a kind of hissing sound that they'd later manipulate to an approximation of a whip-crack.

On another occasion, for 'Blasphemous Rumours', they created a clanking, metallic sound by smashing a hammer against the studio's concrete floor. By then the novelty of sampling industrial sounds had worn off slightly, they weren't heading out to building sites anymore, but they were happy to use whatever came to hand.

The result was easily the best collection of songs Depeche Mode had come up with so far. The lyrically cumbersome 'People Are People' might, significantly, have done better in countries where they didn't speak English as a first language, but it still had a powerful, distinctive melody. The same thing was true of opening track 'Something To Do', whose pulsing urgency belied the rather banal words. It sounded like a traffic jam in a busy city, with hysteria rising.

Perhaps equally important, though, was the band's new found ability to produce slower tracks that still had the power and dynamism of their pop tunes. 'Lie To Me', 'It Doesn't Matter' and 'Stories Of Old' were far more relaxed and confident sounding than anything they'd done before. There was a kind of elegance to them that came from Dave's slow, smooth baritone. Martin was starting to understand what kind of songs worked with Dave's voice.

This cut the other way, too. There were some songs that sounded rather odd with Dave singing them. One such was 'Somebody'. It was a deeply personal track, essentially Martin's own wish-list for the perfect girlfriend. There were many songs that were extremely personal to the songwriter that Dave had sung but this one was so delicate that, when he tried to sing it, his powerful voice made it sound slightly ridiculous. Martin's ambiguous tones worked much better with the song's sentiment, total sincerity hiding behind just the faintest veil of irony.

Equally it would have sounded ridiculous for the songwriter to sing 'Master And Servant'. Their partnership was reaching a new level but it was still entirely unspoken. Martin rarely complained to Dave about anything. If he didn't like something he simply stopped talking. It sometimes seemed as though he needed a mouthpiece. Often Dave and Alan would find out from Fletch that he was unhappy. Equally Dave's voice became the mouthpiece for most of Martin's songs. It made it easier for him to produce broad, brash tunes like 'Master And Servant', safe in the knowledge that he wouldn't be the one singing them.

But he undoubtedly had a hidden exhibitionistic streak of his own. When he came to record 'Somebody' he elected, to Alan's alarm, to do it naked. The two of them set up in the cavernous main hall of Hansa with Alan turning the piano decorously around before Martin started to sing. Meanwhile Dave decided that it would be amusing to send the female tape-op downstairs to "check the connections". He was rewarded a few minutes later by her scream. "If every song had been finished so quickly we'd have made more money out of the album," he said later.

But it was 'Master And Servant' that did the job, once and for all, of stamping on Depeche Mode's clean, safe image. It was a song that they'd struggled to get right. The production and mixing sessions were the longest they'd ever had and, even after a week's work, they famously left out the last snare drum from the final mix. It was a tremendous choice for a single. Dave sang it with a lecherous gusto that brushed over Martin's insistence that the bondage theme was actually a metaphor for inequality in normal life.

When Depeche Mode chose it to be the second single off the album, they were worried about whether anybody would play it. According to legend, Radio One in the UK only played it because the senior staffer who normally made censorship decisions was on holiday. "Somebody did complain to the BBC," said Alan, "but there was someone there intelligent enough to read a copy of the lyrics and actually see a little more in them. That was quite encouraging."

In reality it seems more likely that the success of Frankie Goes To Hollywood's 'Relax' the year before had taught the radio programmers the futility of banning records. The lack of airplay in the US, however, did set Depeche Mode back slightly. 'People Are People' had been their big breakthrough single there, reaching Number 13 but 'Master And Servant' ran aground at 87. Perhaps sensibly, Clive Richardson's video emphasised the song's metaphorical element rather than the S&M theme. It cut footage of the band playing like they're having the best time in the world, with images of ordinary people getting through their work-a-day drudgery. The idea was to show the song's theme of domination in everyday life but it mainly succeeded in showing how much more fun being a pop star is than most other occupations.

If they were worried about censorship, though, it didn't make them change tack. The next single was a double a-side of the

## DEPECHE MODE & THE SECOND COMING

brilliant 'Blasphemous Rumours' and 'Somebody'. 'Blasphemous Rumours', with its story of a 16-year-old girl who slashes her wrists, survives and then goes on to die in a car crash two years later, was almost calculated to get banned in America. The claim that God had a sick sense of humour was bitterly denied by the church.

"If we can say God so loved the world that He sent His only son, if He did that He cannot have a sick sense of humour," a Basildon vicar told Southend's local paper.

But 'Blasphemous Rumours' also went Top 20 in the UK as almost all of their singles had. Clive Richardson's video also provided a crash course in how to make a Depeche Mode song. All you needed, apparently, was a bicycle wheel, a sheet of metal, a large hammer, a pair of scissors and a few saucepans. Out of all that though (and, admittedly, some extremely expensive studio equipment and accompanying wizardry), they'd come up with one of their most enduring melodies.

They'd now become the kind of band who were big without necessarily being recognised as such. They had a loyal fanbase who would buy everything they put out, regardless of whether it got played on the radio or whether their pictures were in magazines. When *Some Great Reward* was released a week after the single on August 27, 1984, it received a far more enthusiastic response from the press than anything they'd done since *Speak And Spell*. "It used to be okay to slag off this bunch because of their lack of soul, their supposed synthetic appeal, their reluctance to really pack a punch," said *Melody Maker*. "*Some Great Reward* just trashes such bad old talk into the ground and demands that you now sit up and take notice of what is happening here, right under your nose."

Almost certainly they would have got better reviews if it wasn't for Martin's lyrics. It did sometimes seem like he would write a great tune and some interesting couplets before torpedoing everything with a spectacularly clunky rhyme. Nevertheless most people were able to overlook this.

"OK, as you've probably guessed, the lyrics look trite, often naïve and frequently clichéd when printed out in industrial grey and white," said Caroline Linfield in *Sounds*. "Yet Depeche have the right balance to pull it off."

*Some Great Reward* duly went Top 5 in the UK and seemed to

vindicate their decision to become an "album band" rather than just a purveyor of great singles. It didn't sell quite as many copies in the UK as their previous albums but greater success in Germany made up for that.

Another indication of the distance they'd travelled came with the release of the *The Singles 81>85*. From 'Dreaming Of Me' to 'Blasphemous Rumours' in four years was pretty astonishing progress. With typical humour, the inlay included a series of quotes from music critics both good and bad. The best, perhaps, was the line, "Deep, meaningful, heavy and arty," which they took from a *Sounds* magazine's review of 'Dreaming Of Me'. The actual review, by Betty Page, read: "Refreshing for its total lack of anything deep, meaningful, heavy or arty."

Another review, by Gary Bushell, declared, "Whether the members of Depeche Mode are actually dead or alive is a question that has baffled the medical profession for years." And, with rather more wit, Neil Tennant of *Smash Hits* said of 'Blasphemous Rumours' that it was "a routine slab of gloom in which God is given a severe ticking off." Neil, of course, would later go on to form the Pet Shop Boys, another synth act occasionally criticised for their dourness that was perhaps helped on its way by bands like Depeche Mode opening the door.

The singles album was inspired by the recording of another track 'Shake The Disease'. Not long after the release of *Some Great Reward*, Depeche Mode went back to Hansa. It was as though now they'd learned how to make the best of the studio, they couldn't keep away. To try and capture its eerie atmosphere, Dave decided to do his vocal in the dark.

"I was terrified," he said. "I had all these noises in my headphones like whispers, and apparently sometimes you can see the shadow of a projectionist up there [in the empty projection box]."

Originally the song was entitled 'Understand Me' but perhaps Martin decided that he'd made enough pleas for understanding after the classic 'Somebody'. The session was intended to be the start of the follow-up to *Some Great Reward,* but they couldn't wait to put it out so they decided to place it on the end of the singles collection along with another track, 'It's Called A Heart'. These weren't the strongest songs they'd ever recorded. On the former, Dave's pitch-black baritone dovetails oddly with a relatively chirpy melody. Both Martin and Alan later said that the latter was one of their least favourite singles and they didn't like the former much, either. They didn't feel they'd had enough time to work on it. "We were touring and trying to do a record at the same time," said Dave. "It was the first single where we had nothing to do with the mixing. It was crying out for a great big chorus but it didn't happen."

This was also the point when they started to think they needed to change their image as well as their music. They'd still yet to produce a video that they were completely happy with. Daniel suggested they hire Peter Care, a director best known for his work with Sheffield's industrial-electronica pioneers Cabaret Voltaire. At the beginning of their career, in the Vince Clarke-era in particular, they'd been highly dubious about the kind of artiness that Cabaret Voltaire personified, but now they were keen on acquiring a little of that edge.

"I think the band flirted for a while with being a little more like Cabaret Voltaire," Peter Care told the author for this book. "I think Cabaret Voltaire was a kind of template for them, the image, the leather jackets, the industrial sounds, the Sheffield-meets-Berlin look. I was aware that I was in danger of ripping off Cabaret Voltaire myself if I wasn't careful. I had to create something different when I was working with Depeche Mode."

Peter wasn't explicitly told by Daniel that they were looking for a change of image but he understood why they'd called him. Their music had changed but their image hadn't. "The one person in Depeche Mode that I felt the most support from was Alan," Peter says. "He came up to me and said very quietly, 'We don't want to look like Basildon guys anymore.' I loved that."

When he came to make the video for 'Shake The Disease', Peter explicitly borrowed from his work with Cabaret Voltaire by re-using the innovative, 'world-upside-down' filming technique that he'd first used in his excellent video for their 'Sensoria' single. Developed by a film-making friend of Peter's, it involved attaching a camera to a rig that swung around in an arc to create the illusion that the Earth was moving. Set in a grimy-looking hotel, the band members appeared to be falling. It was, perhaps, the only part of the video that worked perfectly. The band themselves still looked bored and Peter says they couldn't get it quite right.

"With 'Shake The Disease' I remember being frustrated because I wanted to do something really cool," he says. "The idea was that Dave would wake up in this hotel room and the walls would move around. So the camera was strapped to him and he was moving around in the room and the room itself was also moving. But when I arrived on the set, [some of the crew] had built a set where the walls didn't move at all and that was half the idea right there. That put a lot more stress on the other images of the camera giving the illusion that the Earth is moving around a person."

The band weren't delighted by the results, particularly Dave, who had to have a heavy camera strapped to his body. Nevertheless when they came to record the video for 'It's Called A Heart', they stuck with Peter Care. It might be more accurate to say that Daniel Miller stuck with Peter Care. The band still trusted him and tended to go along with what the record company suggested. At times, though, they had their doubts. They all wanted the vastly superior 'Fly On The Windscreen' to be the next a-side, rather than 'It's Called A Heart' but Mute vetoed it on the grounds that radio wouldn't play a song that began with the line "death is everywhere."

For the 'It's Called A Heart' video, Peter Care did at least give them a more exuberant, energetic image than they'd had before. They were filmed crashing through a cornfield with burning effigies hanging behind them and TV screens hanging from trees. They had no idea what it meant but they threw themselves into the shoot with their usual work ethic.

"I wanted it to feel somewhat tribal," Peter says. "I'd seen a photograph of a tribe in New Guinea or Chad or somewhere like that and after someone had gone to shoot some news-reel footage of them, they made a camera out of pieces of wood. I wanted to use that. I thought that was a pretty great image."

Privately the band were baffled. "Quite how he equated 'calling something a heart' with twirling cameras around on the end of a string in a field of corn in Reading dressed in a skirt, I'll never be able to tell you," Alan later said on the website of his solo project www.recoil.co.uk, "but then," he admitted, "the track was asking for it ... what's it all about, eh?"

The band simply didn't enjoy making videos and often saw them as something to be got over with as quickly as possible. At this point they were just working with the people Daniel suggested and they weren't forming lasting relationships with their collaborators. "I don't know that they wanted to relate to me in that way," says Peter. "It was very much like doing a still shoot for *NME* or something. You turn up for four hours and then go away again. I wasn't looking to make friends."

Perhaps one reason why Mute wanted to go with 'It's Called A Heart' rather than 'Fly On The Windscreen' was that in 1985 the morbid lyrics might have seemed a little too apposite. With famine in Ethiopia having dominated news programmes for much of the previous year, it was something that was impossible to avoid. But when Bob Geldof put together the 'Band Aid' single at the end of 1984 and Live Aid in 1985, Depeche Mode were conspicuous by their absence. It was obviously impossible to admit that if they were miffed. Complaining would have seemed ridiculous but surely they wondered if Geldof had noticed how many records they'd sold internationally by that point. Like many people, they had reservations about pop stars rattling collection boxes at ordinary people, but no doubt they would like to have been asked.

"We weren't asked to do Band Aid," Dave told *Creem* magazine. "The way it was put together was like Bob's-close-friends sort of thing and then it expanded from there and we don't really mix with that crowd. Since then in every interview we've had to explain ourselves, but there were a lot of bands that didn't do it that were pretty upset about it."

"Because we are on an independent label we just don't have the contacts," Andy added to *Blitz* magazine later, "so we weren't asked to appear … at the time we were bitter, but the whole thing has just become so tacky – all those ageing rock bands appearing solely to boost their own career – that in a way we are quite glad we weren't involved. Of course the money raised can't be criticised…"

As this quote shows, they were all fairly contemptuous of the rock star aristocracy that had emerged in the early 1980s. It was, as Neil Tennant, wrote in *Smash Hits*, "as though punk never happened." They were particularly scathing about stars who owned huge houses in Britain but spent much of the year abroad to avoid paying income tax. "It's like the 1970s all these bands living in mansions," said Dave. "If we did that the band would split up. And the money they save on tax they spend on first class airfares. They all come home every weekend!" "They've got no confidence in their own futures," added Fletch astutely. "It's like they're making it while they can. We intend to stay around."

# 8

# CONSOLIDATION

After *Some Great Reward*, Depeche Mode wouldn't make another new album for over a year, a long time for them. In the meantime Dave surprised everybody by getting married to Joanne. By then they'd already been living together for six years and he had all the accoutrements of both a nice domestic life and an Essex boy made good. They lived in a big house in Basildon, he drove a highly exclusive Porsche 911. "I think that if you've got money it's wrong to feel guilty about spending it," he said. "I've always spent what money I've had, whether it be a fiver or five hundred."

He'd got everything he'd ever wanted and it sounded like the decision to ask her to marry him was almost a whim. "One morning, I got up and said to her, 'Do you want to get married?' I virtually said it like that," he recalled later. One rather practical reason he gave for their decision was, "When I go away, which is quite often, Jo needs to sort things out for me, and it helps if she can say 'I'm Mrs Gahan' rather than 'I'm his girlfriend.'"

"Jo's the only girl I've ever met that I could live with," he also said. "I just get on with her. We have lots of arguments just like anybody else but somehow ... we cross over, there's something about it that's special."

The wedding was in a registry office with just immediate family and close friends attending. Fletch was the only representative from the band but Martin and Alan made it to the much bigger party afterwards, along with friends like Alison Moyet and their contemporaries Blancmange. Having had so much success with the band, it seemed that professionally he was fulfilled and was therefore perhaps looking for something else. Also, although he was still young, in Basildon many of his old friends were getting married and having children. Maybe he felt like he was missing out and wanted to create the kind of family life that he'd not had since before his stepfather died.

"I just think it would throw a whole new perspective on life," he said, of starting a family. "Having to bring up a child totally puts aside all the things that were important to you before. Things like being in the band would become secondary."

Dave had told their press officer, not to tell anybody about the wedding. It wasn't a secret that he'd been with Jo for years but he didn't want a big deal made out it. "Obviously, we could have played on it. It doesn't bother me to be in the daily papers but so what? Who cares? Thousands of people get married every day."

It was clearly a case of absence making the heart grow fonder because the *Some Great Reward* tour was the longest Depeche Mode had done, with 87 dates, and Dave was rarely at home. They did at least play four nights at the Hammersmith Odeon but the biggest surprise was to find out that, by now, they had a big following in America.

"Until about 1985, we honestly felt that we never had a hope in hell of doing well in America," Fletch said to *Revolver*. "We felt our music sounded ridiculously too European, and our look was too European. Hence, we didn't do any work in America for three years. Then out of nowhere, we announced a tour, and it sold out immediately."

"We went to America in 1982 and 1983 and we got a very negative response from journalists," said Martin. "We were playing to about 1,000 people every night. We sort of gave up on America at that time. We thought our music just wasn't suited. But when we went back in 1985 we noticed a really big change in opinion. Everybody's attitude seemed to have changed suddenly. We seemed to be accepted and from that time on we just built gradually."

Their fans in America had a different attitude to their British fans, too. They weren't aware of Depeche Mode's early incarnation as a teen pop band. They hadn't seen the pictures in *Smash Hits*. Their idea of the band had been formed during the edgy, sexually ambiguous Berlin period and they thought of them as cool, dark European deviants. It was an image that struck a chord and seemed highly exotic from the viewpoint of places like Kansas and Ohio.

"When we were in Texas," Fletch said, "this girl rang up our room and after talking quite a bit, she said 'When I put on your records it's like listening to a slice of Europe', which is great because I think you can't relate our music to any American style at all."

But those fans who actually met the band must have found them much more down-to-Earth than they expected. Occasionally they arrived expecting to have deep conversations about philosophy. Even back in 1982 Dave had occasionally found himself having to live up to the expectations of American fans. "The really embarrassing moments are in America because we seem to attract musical aficionados or the intellectual side of the business, which is really strange," he said to *Zig Zag*. "In Britain we're very well known and have a huge following who are of the usual type ... lots of young girls, naturally. But in the States we don't receive that kind of reaction at all. People who come backstage or to our gigs tend to be much more upmarket. It's quite weird and we don't know how to react to it!"

After America there were festival dates in Europe and the reaction was even more extreme there. At one gig in Florence Dave said later he thought he was going to have a heart attack. They were playing inside a tent and it was so hot that steam was rising from the stage and it was raining condensation. "I remember not being able to breathe because there wasn't any air," he said. "Pretty heavy gig!"

On that tour they also made the unusual decision to play gigs behind the Iron Curtain in Budapest and Warsaw. They had no idea what to expect. They had no record sales in those countries and, because it was illegal to take money out of Poland or Hungary, there was no chance they could make a profit playing there. They just went because they could. The response staggered them.

They couldn't walk the streets without being mobbed. In some ways it was the worst kind of fame because they, inevitably, didn't sell many records behind the Iron Curtain. Most fans made do with bootlegs and tapes. Far more people knew their music than they were expecting and the arenas – Volan Stadion in Budapest and Towar Hall in Warsaw – had an explosive atmosphere. In Hungary, particularly, some fans had an attention to detail which could be disconcerting.

"In Hungary there are actually groups of fans called 'Depeches'!" Dave told Paul Lester of *Sky* magazine in 1990. "They're like the mods and rockers we get in Britain, our hotel was surrounded by them, and they all looked like one of us. We'd go out there and it would be like looking at loads of mirrors, all these kids copying our image – not that we have a particularly strong image, really. So there'd be loads of Martins and Alans and Daves and Andys, and we literally couldn't go anywhere without being mobbed by these so-called 'Depeches'." It was an exciting experience but also something of a culture shock. "They'd obviously got hold of the music," he continued. "But it was depressing seeing all those people who were very frustrated and wanted to see more bands and there aren't many bands that go there."

They'd tried to book gigs in Russia and East Germany but although these proved impossible to arrange, it was the start of a relationship with their fans in the old 'Eastern Bloc' that would be much deeper than they'd ever expected. "In the 1980s, Depeche Mode was to Russia what Elvis was to 1950s America," said artist Jeremy Deller who made a film *The Posters Came From The Walls* about their fans. "At the beginning, tapes circulated secretly. Then they became this cult."

For Dave it was particularly strange. He still regarded himself very much as an ordinary Basildon boy yet he was the object of much of the fans' adulation. To many fans in Russia, the National Holiday, Victory Day, on May 9, was later better known as "Dave Day", because it happened to be Dave Gahan's birthday. Every year in Moscow fans gather to sing Depeche Mode songs and celebrate his life. "I don't think there's another lead singer in the world who has the kind of following that Dave Gahan of Depeche Mode enjoys in Russia," Jeremy said in *The Guardian*. "It's like a benevolent cult."

The fans in Poland and Hungary were delighted that Depeche Mode had come when so few bands ever bothered but at the same time there would be a certain frustration in the years ahead that it took them so long to go back. This was simply because they now had fans all over the world. It was impossible for them to play to everybody who wanted to see them. In 1985 they also made their first trip to Greece, for a festival near Athens. That too was a disconcerting experience. The festival was put on by the Government and, perhaps as a result, it attracted attention from anarchists determined to cause trouble.

They were playing to a highly volatile crowd of 80,000 people along with The Clash, The Cure and Culture Club, who were headlining. Their set went down extremely well, much better than that of Culture Club. But outside on the streets anarchists were demanding free entry. The next day Dave was going shopping when somebody punched him in the face.

Significantly, perhaps, Jo didn't tend to come on tour with the band in the mid-1980s as she'd done at the beginning. In one very early Q+A interview, Dave had said that she "mostly" came with them, adding, "we, in Depeche Mode, give no credence to the assertion that women always cause trouble in a band. Andrew's girlfriend, Grainne, mostly joins us on tour too and it's social most of the time."

But by 1985 he'd changed his mind.

"She can come, but it doesn't work," he told *Record Mirror*. "It's very difficult. I'm a totally different person on tour. I can be really horrible 'cos I'm so locked into what I do. When Jo's there, I like it, but if she's there every day and if I'm feeling in a bad mood, I just take it out on her. We've had screaming fights like that."

At the start of Depeche Mode, Dave, Martin and Fletch's girlfriends had all been heavily involved in helping them get off the ground. Joanne had run the fan-club but eventually Dave asked her to stop. "It all just got a bit too big," he said to *No 1*. "I'd come home, and there would be posters and records everywhere – all I wanted was a break! I just couldn't handle it. I just couldn't get away from Depeche Mode. It got to the stage where we didn't talk anymore. She'd just ask me questions like: 'What colour socks were you wearing that night in Berlin?'"

By the time they went back to Hansa in November 1985, the domestic Dave Gahan was already starting to lose ground to the inner hedonist. He'd always liked to be part of things. Sitting on the outside while other people partied didn't suit him at all. Years later he'd say that he felt like he was living a lie at this time. When everybody thought he was the clean-cut young husband, he was partying hard. "During the 1980s, we were out drinking and tooting it up, like everybody," he told *Q*.

But they were also growing up and starting to demand greater control over matters. For the first time they asked Daniel to draw up a contract for the relationship between Depeche Mode and the record label. Another reason, perhaps, for finally signing was that relationships within the group were struggling.

"If ever we were going to split up the band," Dave said to *Melody Maker* in 1990, "it was at the end of 1985. We were really in a state of turmoil. Constant arguing. Very intense. We weren't really sure where to go after *Some Great Reward* so we decided to slow things down. But it left us with too much time on our hands. So we spent most of our time arguing. Sometimes, it seems incredible that we came out of that period with the band and our sanity intact."

The nature of the band caused difficulties. Because they didn't have a manager or any single dominant member everything they did had to get past four separate vetoes, or five if you included Daniel Miller. "We have to have a row about every little decision," Fletch breezily admitted in one TV interview. They were unusual in that Dave and Martin were almost like two halves of the normal frontman. In most bands the person who writes and sings the songs will usually have the final say but Depeche Mode were based on mutual dependency. As they'd got bigger it became increasingly difficult for them to have the kind of control that they were now demanding.

One change that would be significant in the future was the recruitment of Jonathan Kessler, initially as a tour accountant. He was just 22-years old and they hired him because, as things had got bigger and bigger, it wasn't possible for Fletch to deal with everything. As time went on, though, he would become the band's, and Dave in particular's, close friend and adviser. He was the person they could talk to and that was no small thing in a band where that person was often hard to find. That he was also a prodigiously gifted business and legal brain was obviously also a superb bonus. He has proved to be one of the band's staunchest allies.

When they went back into Hansa in November 1985, they were a very different unit than the fresh-faced pop kids of four years previously. They had the security of a hardcore fanbase waiting to hear what they would come up with. They didn't need to write instant hits to grab their fans' attention. They could make the kind of slow-burning music that, ever since Vince left, they'd said they wanted. This was the period that really defined Depeche Mode and set them up for their megastardom …

## DEPECHE MODE & THE SECOND COMING

… yet, at the time, things weren't that easy …

There was a power struggle going on within the band as they tried to decide upon their new direction. An era was drawing to a close and a new one was starting as Alan Wilder began to take more interest in the production side of things. This was at a time when the production, the texture of the records, was becoming more and more important. The first product of the new Hansa sessions, the single 'Stripped', contained some of the most innovative sampling they'd done. On November 5, for example, they celebrated Guy Fawkes Day by heading outside and firing rockets in the car park. Microphones underneath captured the sound of them whizzing past as the band ducked for cover. "That was probably the most dangerous bit of sampling we've ever done," Daniel said later.

They then added a distorted motorbike engine for the beat and included the roar of Dave's Porsche at the beginning. It was almost the archetypal Depeche Mode track. It had everything that you'd associate with the band at that time and, like 'Master And Servant' before it, 'Stripped' used sexual imagery to make a wider point about society.

"It's about two people trying to get back to nothing, just living off the land," Dave said in a TV interview after the release. "It's not like 'Take your clothes off,' although a lot of people took it like that." Fletch added: "You can take it like that if you want to."

The video, the last that Peter Care would direct for the band, carefully avoided that interpretation. It was by far the best work he'd done for Depeche Mode, featuring them smashing up a car with hammers and then carrying giant TV screens across the street. They filmed it near Hansa as curious East German border guards looked on from the Berlin Wall. Nevertheless Peter still wasn't sure that the band were convinced by what he was doing. He felt that Dave, in particular, was dubious about his work. The singer, who'd studied fashion at college, had very strong ideas about his own image.

"By the time I did 'Stripped', I felt like Alan was into working with me but I'm not sure the others were," Peter says. "I don't think David enjoyed working with me that much. Whatever he needed as a lead singer, the kind of heterosexual, sexy leader of the band, as it were, wasn't there. There wasn't tension, there just wasn't any particular empathy."

But he did notice a certain tension emerging between what Dave wanted and what Martin and Fletch wanted. "I felt it when I was working on 'Stripped', he says. "They'd just done a tremendously successful concert and they had some footage of thousands of people holding cigarette lighters and waving them in the air. Dave wanted that included in the video. It was probably a nice memory for him but I couldn't see how it fitted in with what the video was about and I just thought, *Oh, they're going to be stadium rock stars now*. I could imagine that would create some kind of tension in the band because I didn't get the feeling that was where Martin and Andy wanted to go. I got the feeling they wanted to be more underground and cool that way."

'Stripped' was released on February 10, 1986, and it followed the same path as most of their singles in the mid-1980s. It rocketed into the Top 20 in the UK, as their enthusiastic hardcore fan-base rushed out and bought it, but then it disappeared. In Germany, of course, it went Top 5. Still, Daniel Miller was concerned that, as they'd matured, they might be giving up writing the kind of pop hits they'd had in the past. Mute were a label that gave artists space to do all kinds of experimentation and yet that depended on the ability of their poppier acts to keep delivering commercially. When he heard the rest of the songs that they wanted for their next album, *Black Celebration*, he was even more concerned.

# 9

# CELEBRATION

Daniel Miller once compared Depeche Mode's Berlin albums to the way famous and infamous German film director Werner Herzog made movies, by pushing the cast and the crew to their absolute limit. In the past this was something he'd wholeheartedly enjoyed but the problems that had surfaced when they made *Some Great Reward* were now growing. With every record it was getting harder for him to justify spending weeks in Depeche Mode's Berlin bubble.

The thing that made them such a great band – their very different personalities – was also the source of the tension. On later albums their roles were all very clearly defined but on *Black Celebration* they were still in flux. It made for a fractious atmosphere at times. They were all arguing and they weren't sure what would happen next.

Still, despite their problems, there was also a kind of freedom in Hansa. The grand, oppressive building might have suited Martin's grand, oppressive songs but they also had a life there that was very Basildon. It wasn't the case that they spent all their time arguing or making intense music. There were regular games of pool, football and even cricket. The band and crew could, at times, be surprisingly competitive. Prog-rockers Marillion once recalled losing to Depeche Mode in a pool tournament. A football match against their German record company had even more painful consequences for the losers. Depeche Mode not only won easily but one of their opponents ended up with a broken leg. On their 'Get Well Soon' card, according to Alan Wilder, they added the laddish coda "45, 66 … 85".

Equally the initial stages of recording could be highly enjoyable, particularly for Dave whose vocals were now reaching a new level. He would often record them on the landing outside the main studio where they would echo against the ceiling. As the record developed, they had the exhilarating feeling that musically they could do what they liked now. They weren't tied to any particular pop formula and they were gleefully dismissive of any controversy that might result from their songs. If 'Fly On The Windscreen' had shocked people, that was nothing compared with the brilliant, seedy 'A Question Of Time', which wrenched open the darkest areas of the male libido. It was a song whose lyrics were highlighted by some in the media, such as *Record Mirror*, as being on the face of it about feeling protective towards an underage girl. The words do seem horribly open about the song's protagonist's feelings. Most people would have sung it tentatively or even awkwardly. That's perhaps how Martin would have sung it; Dave, however, plunges into it with a fictional relish that does more to bring out the song's theme of the greedy male libido than any delicate interpretation. This lack of self-consciousness is what makes him such a great interpreter of Martin's lyrics. Here, as elsewhere, he is an actor. Whether he was being asked to sing a terrible rhyming couplet or a deeply complex and dark song like 'A Question Of Time', he was able to deliver it absolutely straight without a shred of self-doubt.

Another example was 'Dressed In Black', a song which harked back to the pre-pop era. It could almost have been on the soundtrack of *Cabaret*. Since living in Germany, Martin had become inspired by composers like the darkly romantic Kurt Weill. It was a long way removed from The Damned or The Clash and yet Dave Gahan sings it like he was born to tread the boards.

*Black Celebration* is more Martin's album than any other Depeche Mode record except, perhaps, *Exciter*. It contains four tracks with his lead vocals and some of his most personal lyrics. Yet the demos he'd produced in 1985 pushed them all to a higher level. They also re-recorded 'Fly On The Windscreen' from the year before, adding, among other things, a sample of the Mute boss saying "horse" very quickly.

For Daniel Miller, though, the *Black Celebration* sessions were a time of huge doubt. He didn't think they'd got the kind of hit single that would make the record sell and he was frustrated by the frequent bickering. "There were quite a lot of arguments going on around that time," Martin said to *Uncut*. "We'd overdone the working relationship between Daniel and Gareth Jones. That was the third album we'd done together and I think everybody'd become very lazy, relying on formulas."

# DEPECHE MODE & THE SECOND COMING

Martin intimated in some interviews that he would have taken the band further towards a dark, heavy sound but the rest of them held him back. Although he could cope with the democratic process much better than Vince Clarke, he still found it difficult to accept. He would give them his demos and he wasn't always convinced that they'd become what he envisaged.

"I've been trying to get away from the softness of contemporary pop," he told Max Bell. "But I know we'll never really go far enough. Depeche Mode is a democracy and it stops me writing what I really want to write."

Nevertheless, he rarely actually told Dave or Alan that. At least not at the time. "We get our say in the studio," Dave said. "Sometimes Martin's not entirely happy with what's happened to his demos, but he's the kind of bloke that doesn't say much till after it's released."

The title of the record captured this period's strange mixture of darkness and joy. They'd made the album at the height of a Berlin winter in an atmosphere that alternated between creativity and distrust. *Black Celebration*, then, was the clearest articulation of their ethos yet. It was all about bringing joy and communion out of the darkest elements of life. This was what touched a chord with so many of the band's fans when it was released. As Dave put it, "at the end of a working day, you go out and drown your sorrows, no matter how shitty you feel or how bleak your future looks."

At the end of the sessions for *Black Celebration*, things looked rather bleak for the band themselves. After a final series of arguments, Martin disappeared when they were mixing the record, heading off to stay with an old school exchange friend in northern Germany. At times Alan wondered how the band had got this far. He said that when he first met them he was shocked at their apparent lack of confidence. The driving forces had often been Vince and Daniel. Since then they'd matured enormously but, even by 1985, they were still in the process of deciding what kind of a band they were going to be. They were still going through the kind of discussions that many young bands have in garages and rehearsal rooms before anybody has heard of them. Yet *Black Celebration* consolidated their image and told the world exactly what kind of a band they were. The sleeve of the record bore the legend: "Life In The So-Called Space Age", a comment, with its dry cynicism, that epitomised Martin's aim of writing music that was rooted in day-to-day life.

It was an album that is still often considered the 'real' fan's favourite. This is partly because their other career peak – *Violator* – brought them to a mass audience while *Black Celebration* seemed to encapsulate everything that they were about at the time. Despite its supposed lack of singles, it combines great tunes with a deeply idiosyncratic world view. It combines experimentation with a pop sensibility that they found impossible to lose. If *Some Great Reward* was the album where they discovered what Depeche Mode was, and the later *Music For The Masses* proved to be the album where they precision tooled it for the world at large, then *Black Celebration* still sounded like the raw product of their peculiar chemistry. Despite all the technology they used, it sounded like a band playing in the studio. Even the moments that misfired slightly, like the clunky 'New Dress' give it a very human feel. It's ironic that synth bands were often criticised for the supposed lack of emotion in their music; Depeche Mode, at this time, always sounded much warmer than the 1980s rock bands who were their contemporaries. But then another strength that they had was their complete detachment from whatever else was going on in the world of pop. When *Black Celebration* arrived, a month after 'Stripped', it didn't take them to a new commercial level but it did inspire new levels of devotion in their hardcore fans. And, by word of mouth, they were becoming bigger and bigger.

The first single to be released following *Black Celebration* was the excellent 'A Question Of Lust' in April 1986. Unsurprisingly it followed the usual Depeche Mode path of being a big hit in Germany and some other countries in Europe, then Top 20 in the UK. The next single 'A Question Of Time' might have been expected to cause more of a stir. Its controversial subject matter could easily have been frothed up into a scandal in the tabloids. At times Depeche Mode might have resented the fact that they were generally ignored by the mainstream press but they were probably lucky here. It's hard to imagine a band like Pulp, say, who actually sold far fewer records a few years later, getting away with a song like that without being excoriated in the tabloids.

Luckily they had a new weapon in their armoury: Anton Corbijn.

## DEPECHE MODE & THE SECOND COMING

Until relatively recently Anton had been best known really as a stills photographer. He'd worked for *NME* for a long time and, of course, took the famous cover shot with Dave Gahan blurred out. In the last couple of years, though, he'd started directing music videos and they asked him if he'd be interested in doing 'A Question Of Time'. Initially he wasn't sure. He'd turned them down twice in the past and only agreed to work with them this time, he said, because they were filming in America and he'd never been there before.

It was an inspired decision all round. The video perfectly brings out the song's darkness and its cheekiness with Anton's very Dutch sense of humour. In grainy black and white, it features a motorbike courier delivering babies down an iconic American highway to the bemused looking band. With all due respect to the excellent work of Clive Richardson and Peter Care, it was by far the best video the band had done to date.

Afterwards, though, Anton said it was a difficult experience. Depeche Mode hated making videos and they didn't make it particularly easy for him. "It was the first time I did my own camera work," he said in an interview with DM's *Bong* fanzine. "There was no money for anything and, apart from Alan, the band only wanted to turn up for three hours."

When he'd finished, he didn't hear from them for months and wondered whether they'd liked it. In fact they were delighted. It was the start of a partnership that would shape their image more than anything else had done so before. Peter Care says he understood why the partnership was so successful. Video shoots are often excruciatingly dull for bands and so they tend to cling to anybody who can make them bearable and interesting.

"I've always felt bad for bands," he says. "I used to think, *Man, all these video directors and producers and companies, they're all middle-class public school boys*, and then the bands were mostly working-class. There was this strange division there. But I always tried to make the shoot interesting for the band and not keep them hanging around. I think a lot of bands [in the 1980s] felt that things were out of their control, nothing was really discussed properly. They had to work with directors they didn't like because of the record company, or the BBC or whatever, making stipulations. I think that's why Depeche

# DAVE GAHAN

Mode ended up working with Anton for so long, and did so brilliantly with him, because they felt like he was one of them. He wasn't working for the Beeb."

For Dave Gahan, in particular, Anton made a huge difference. He'd often despaired of his band's image. From the cheap suits of the early days to Martin's leather miniskirts of the previous year he thought that they rarely got it right. As a fashion student he'd always been very conscious of how they looked. After all the different styles they'd been through, they ended up going back to the black leather look that they'd worn in their early days. It was a very Berlin image.

"We went through a period where we'd worn suits to go with songs like 'See You' which I think was the worst period," Dave said. "But before, when we first started, we were wearing leather, basically the leather gay look. That was from most of our friends. It was our best look."

Way back in November 1980, the *Basildon Echo* illustrated an early news story with the headline 'Posh Clobber Could Clinch It For Mode.' It made its way on to the inlay of their first singles collection as an example of the kind of cheesy press that they'd had at the beginning but it was, in a funny way, very prescient. Depeche Mode's image problems didn't do them much harm in Germany and certain other European countries but they didn't help in the UK.

Anton often captured their dark, fetishistic look with his videos and in the photographs he took of them but, crucially, there was also a distinct sense of humour. He had a certain aesthetic which was instantly recognisable. Dave almost certainly liked the fact that the director used him as the star of Depeche Mode videos much more often than their previous directors had. If there was any 'acting' to be done then he was the one to do it and he managed far better than he had in the past. Essentially Anton just let the frontman's natural charisma do the work without asking him to do anything that looked awkward.

"I felt really comfortable with Anton," Dave said in *Uncut* in 2001. "He was trying to portray us in a good light. It wasn't like it was just a job, he definitely was in it for the long term." Their whole career had been a definitive lesson in doing things for the long term. Instead of taking short-cuts and going for easy money, they'd built things up slowly. *Black Celebration* was another example of that. It had seemed to flop by most 1980s pop bands' standards. There were no Top 10 hits in the UK or the USA and they weren't all over the radio. Somehow, though, when they started selling tickets for *The Black Celebration Tour,* they found that they were bigger than ever. The tour saw them playing to 10,000 or more people in some cities in America, despite the fact that they'd never even had an album in the Top 100 there.

In England, shockingly for what was now an 'alternative' band, they were playing two nights at Wembley Arena. "I imagine some fans are a bit cross that we're doing Wembley," said Martin, "but we have to break out of this credibility thing. I thought The Cure doing Wembley was brilliant and I know I need large crowds these days to excite me."

Depeche Mode were in the fortunate position of being everybody's favourite secret. They were far removed from the mainstream and yet they had enough fans to be able to command huge audiences. When they went to the States they were often warned "not to go Top 40". It was thought that it would be the death of their credibility if they became a chart hit band. When 'Everything Counts' went Top 40, then, they'd been a little worried. How could they avoid going into the charts if the radio started playing their singles and people bought them? But, by accident or by design, songs like 'Blasphemous Rumours' and 'Stripped' meant they'd become the definitive cult band. It was a time, too, when cult bands could become enormous. Acts like The Cure were selling more and more records despite their 'alternative' label.

"I think we're in a weird position, in Britain we're very much out on our own," said Dave to *Record Mirror*, "whereas in Germany, France and in Italy we've got very much the same audience as 'new wave' bands like The Cure. In Britain, I don't think there are that many people buying Cure records who also buy Depeche Mode records. It's all down to our 'pop' tag and our background."

In a sense they were more like Britain's big metal bands such as Iron Maiden and Judas Priest than they were their pop contemporaries. Those bands, too, weren't taken that seriously in Britain and yet sold vast quantities overseas. They also had devoted fan-bases in every town who could be spotted in their black t-shirts.

It was a connection they noticed. In a Danish interview they laughingly dubbed their music "electronic metal" and Martin joked: "Heavy metal's in at the moment. Our music's like subtle heavy. They're slow ballads but they're still heavy."

Gareth Jones had made this connection clear a couple of years before with the 'metal mix' of their song 'Something To Do' on the b-side of 'Shake The Disease', which brought out the song's chaotic energy and turned everything up to eleven. This was the kind of thing that Dave, who'd grown up with the distorted rock energy of The Damned and The Clash, loved. Although he was also a big soul fan, his preference when they played live was always for songs that allowed him to rock out a little. His live performances were becoming increasingly energetic by then and, in 1986, he was already starting to wonder whether they were playing too often to sustain that intensity.

"The fewer gigs you do on a tour the more you enjoy yourself," he said. "I love the audience contact, it gives me a big kick that you can't get in the studio or on TV – I always feel a great deal of power when I can make 6,000 people do what I want."

There was also a problem that the feelings he had on stage were impossible to replicate off-stage and it was very difficult to adjust after a tour. "Telling 9,000 people what to do is like being on another planet," he said, but the experience could often be bad for his health, both physically and mentally. The whole band found it gruelling at times but Dave, who ran around the stage every night while they stood behind their synths, felt it hardest.

"I lose one and a half stone on every tour," he said to *No 1*. "I travel with a full medicine bag, vitamins, blood cell restorers, glycerine and antibiotics. I tend to get quite ill on tour. When I'm home I speed round the house for months trying to adapt to normality, things like paying bills and going to the launderette become very hard."

It was difficult for Joanne, too. Since they'd got married Dave had been away for a huge amount of time. The band's success was partly built upon their willingness to tour endlessly but it was taking a lot out of them personally. The actual shows, though, impressed even their cynical British critics who were belatedly realising what a phenomenon they were. Their Wembley show received

## DEPECHE MODE & THE SECOND COMING

a particularly gratifying review from John Peel, who'd first played 'Photographic' at the start of their career.

"If we are to have bands filling the world's stadiums," he said, "then let them be like Depeche Mode." The fact that they were so much bigger as a live act than as recording artists was not what Dave had envisaged when they started. In an early interview he once said that he didn't think that most of their fans were the kind of people who went to gigs, they just bought records.

The band's greater success brought its own problems. Fans had discovered Dave's address in Basildon and eventually he was forced to move because he'd wake up and there would be kids outside his window. "I'd get kids coming from all over the world," he said to *NME* in 1990, "Germany, France, America – they'd just hang out at the end of my drive. It got to the point where I'd be chasing them down the road with my dog because they'd be singing our songs outside my house at two in the morning."

This kind of thing started to seem more alarming when Joanne discovered at the beginning of 1987 that she was pregnant. Between the end of the *Black Celebration* tour in August 1986 and going back in to the studio in February 1987, they at last had some time together and it seemed like Dave really could be domestic, do the "Essex thing", as his friends put it.

But it wouldn't be long before Depeche Mode would be taking him away somewhere again, whether he liked it or not.

# 10

# MUSIC FOR THE MASSES

The title of Depeche Mode's next album, *Music For The Masses,* was supposed to be semi-ironic. They didn't think of themselves as a big band. They were on a 'little indie label' and they'd yet to have more than a sole Top 5 single in the UK. Their songs were about death, religious guilt and weird sex, so they weren't exactly conducive to mainstream play on the radio. The enthusiasm of their dedicated fan-base was now almost working against them. Every time they released a single, their fans would buy it in the first week and then it would disappear.

"We felt that was part of the problem," said Dave in 1990. "Other people weren't getting the chance to hear about Depeche Mode and a chance to enjoy it or dislike it or whatever because it was over within three weeks. In the past, songs would be around for eight to ten weeks but you can't control that anymore. You can't control how many people are going to buy your record in the first week." They appeared to have reached a plateau – albeit a relatively high one – but a plateau none the less. This was the reason for the album title.

"People assumed that the title was a kind of arrogance on our part," Dave said. "But it was a total joke. We felt at the time that our music would never cross over to the general public. We thought we were on the edge between commercial and non-commercial and that's the way it should stay."

Although they decided to make some changes, bringing in a new producer, Dave Bascombe, and recording away from Hansa for the first time since 1983, *Music For The Masses* would be a continuation, in many ways, of *Black Celebration*. This time, though, they went to Paris, to the Guillame Tell studio in Pigalle, the red light district. Although it was very different to Berlin, it had a similarly seamy vibe. They'd wanted to work in the city for many years but Guillame Tell was the first place they'd found that had the kind of technical facilities they needed, combined with an inspiring atmosphere.

It wasn't quite what they were used to but Paris certainly had its own unique charm.

"We used it say it was like a video game," said Martin. "You know, on one side you'd be trying to dodge the drunks and on the other side people would be grabbing you to go in to see the strippers. And, for some reason, there were always dog turds all over the street."

They were also surprised by the behaviour of the French fans. They'd never regarded the country as real Depeche Mode territory, despite or because of their French name. They didn't sell the same quantities of records there than they did in Germany, or play such big venues. But the fans were as rabid as any they'd seen.

"The French fans are unbelievable," Dave told *Smash Hits*. "They sit outside the recording studio and if any of us come out they all barge up going, 'Was that eet? Was that the seengle vee just heard? Was eet the seengle?'"

The first fruit of the sessions was the single, 'Strangelove', which arrived very early in April 1987. It was a promising sign. While it continued the themes of *Black Celebration*, it had their most naggingly insistent chorus since 'Master And Servant'. They released it while still working on the album and it became their first single since 'Everything Counts' to chart in America.

On the video, with typical Dutch directness, Anton didn't try and pretend that the song was actually about industrial relations or the Cold War. It's a very French affair with assorted sultry models pouting at the band alongside their new logo, a megaphone arranged as a kind of phallic symbol. Endearingly, towards the end, both models and band are shown cracking up with laughter. It was an image that probably summed up his new take on their aesthetic.

In the UK and in Europe, 'Strangelove' followed the same pattern as all their singles. By now it was almost as though there was a subset of society who would always buy Depeche Mode singles, while the rest of the country paid little attention. Perhaps unwisely, they tried to address this problem by throwing a party for a *Smash Hits* magazine feature. The idea seems to have been to counter their new serious, gloomy image by showing them as the party-loving band that they really were. It worked, up to a point. Journalist Sylvia Patterson duly reported in *Smash Hits*' characteristically bright, funny style, that they were, indeed, fun-loving chaps.

"Depeche Mode are the friendliest, happiest pop stars that ever existed," she reported. Unsurprisingly they all let their guard down and by the end of the night she was reporting that a rather inebriated Andy was saying, "Quite honestly I only do this for the money. For the money and the memories, the money and the memories." Meanwhile Alan said, "I suppose you think that we all get on really well together and it's like this all the time – well, it isn't!"

Even allowing for the fact that these were obviously just drunken comments at the end of a long evening, it wasn't exactly how the band wanted to be portrayed. Still, it was far more revealing than most 'serious' interviews. They were shown as a band who did indeed know how to party but also one that occasionally had doubts about what they were doing. Later on this was one of many magazine articles that they had regrets about doing, Alan in particular.

But despite the fact that there were obviously problems within the band, things were improving after the low point of *Black Celebration*. They were in the studio for another four months after the release of 'Strangelove' and the atmosphere was much better than it had been during their last sessions at Hansa. Martin said they were like a "gang" again. The resulting album would be the last to have the clanking, industrial sound of their Berlin years and it was a fitting full-stop on that period. After *Music For The Masses*, their production budget rose drastically but there's something endearing about the fact that the edges hadn't been knocked off. They were still working with their own, very DIY samples. 'I Want You Now', for example, featured an accordion being inflated and deflated to create an eerie breathing sound. It also featured two girls who just happened to be hanging around the studio adding sighs and giggles.

If *Black Celebration* had been short of singles, *Music For The Masses* very much redressed the balance. There were numerous tracks that could, potentially, have been released. 'Never Let Me Down Again' is a pop song with its industrial framework still showing, 'Strangelove' was an instant pop classic and 'Behind The Wheel' was probably Martin's most subtle rumination on one of his favourite lyrical themes. On 'Never Let Me Down Again' he even threw in one of his ridiculous lyrical clunkers, rhyming 'houses' and 'trousers' to amuse the critics and challenge Dave's powers of maintaining a straight face.

*Music For The Masses* was an album with a sharper, more defined sound than any of their previous efforts. It had a sense of direction and a feeling that they knew exactly what they were doing. Afterwards they'd feel the need to tear up the blueprint to stop things from getting boring but right now they were absolutely on top of their game. It made the synth-pop tag irrelevant because it had everything that was good about rock 'n' roll; most importantly gigantic, sing-a-long choruses and a colossal backbeat. Their music wasn't arena rock but it had been shaped by playing in arenas. They'd learned what worked and what didn't in front of audiences of thousands of people. They were increasingly cutting anything out that couldn't appeal to the back-row of an enormodrome. Many people, not the least the band themselves, thought they'd peaked with *Music For The Masses*. It was hard to see what else they had to say.

This was the album where critics in the UK started to come around to the idea that this was a band with substance. In *NME* Jane Solanas said that, "If you still think Depeche Mode are beneath adult consideration, consider this: their music has been turned into tape-loops by experimental underground Soviet groups and hi-jacked as backing tracks by Chicago House producers."

And in *Record Mirror* Eleanor Levy pointed out that the relative failure of 'Behind The Wheel' could be a sign that they were at last losing their old pop fans with their move towards a darker sound. "Common consensus among all, bar the record-buying public, would have it that this latest D Mode 45 is perhaps the best thing they have ever done," she said. "The fact is that this dark, sensual track is probably far too disturbing for the Rick Astley fans among us and though it points to a more mature Depeche Mode, it may well be the beginning of the end of the common misconception that they are a 'girly synthesiser' band. Features in 'serious' music papers may have come and gone, but only stark chart failure will finally secure one of the most consistent bands of the last few years a place in the hall of 'credible chart' fame."

This wasn't quite true but *Music For The Masses*, if it didn't exactly fail in the charts, certainly didn't pull in many new fans. It was just bought by the people who always bought their records. However years later the www.depechemode.tv website ran a feature claiming, perhaps with some justification, that it was the combination of 'Behind The Wheel' and its b-side, a cover of 'Route 66' that made them so popular in California.

"Both connected with Southern California's auto driven culture in 1988," they commented. "Already 'riding high' with the fan-base on the last two releases, this release was the final cement that bound the band with their rabid LA fan base. They were always close to the region over the years, but with this release, they had seemingly taken residency somewhere in the valley."

*Music For The Masses* was released at the end of September 1987 and then, with impeccable timing, Dave's son Jack Gahan was born less than a month later. Eight days after that Depeche Mode were off on tour. This was where *Music For The Masses* really made sense.

It was a period that he would always feel guilty about. The tour lasted for nine months and Dave had long since given up pretending that he got his kicks from fishing and domestic bliss. "I felt like shit because I constantly cheated on my wife," he admitted to *Q* in 2005. "I went home and lied, my soul needed cleansing badly."

Sleeping with a groupie didn't necessarily help him feel good about himself, either. Part of the appeal was simply about being wanted but he quickly learned that they were using him just as much as he was using them. It could sometimes be a chastening experience. He had some particularly humbling moments in Japan. "You think you're their favourite," he said to *Rolling Stone* years later, "then after you've kind of, you know, engaged in the debauchery, they will pull out photo albums of all their other conquests. And suddenly, to your horror, you see pictures of just about every other band that went to Japan over the past ten years … every band you could think of. And you're like, 'Whoa! OK, so I'm not special.'"

Even if they still didn't sell millions of records, Depeche Mode were suddenly bigger than they'd ever been. The *Music For The Masses* tour would dwarf all the others and they would spend half of 1988 on the road. This included a date on the other side of the Berlin Wall for the first time, in front of 6,000 East Berliners. Perhaps

## DEPECHE MODE & THE SECOND COMING

if they'd known a little more about who was organising it they wouldn't have gone but Depeche Mode were still essentially naïve in their politics. They just wanted to play to people who wanted to see them. The show was officially a birthday party for the "FDJ" – Freie Deutsche Jugend – or Free German Youth. They were an organisation set up to promote Marxist-Leninist values among the young people of East Germany. Tickets, then, were only available to kids who were considered "good" students, regardless of whether or not they were fans of the band. This meant many real fans ended up paying vast sums of money to buy the tickets off those "good" students.

Afterwards the band had mixed memories of the show. "Even when we did the soundcheck there was about 800 police in there," said Fletch in a 2008 press conference, "and we found out afterwards that most of the audience were members of the security forces or whatever. The real fans were kept five or six miles from the gig."

In 1988 they also decided to pay back a debt to a band who'd been an influence on Martin, in particular, from the beginning – Orchestral Manoeuvres In The Dark. It was a mixed blessing for OMD. They were able to play to huge audiences every night but they had to watch while the band who they'd influenced rake in money while they followed along in their wake. It didn't help that relations between them were occasionally tense. Alan Wilder wasn't keen on OMD's frontman Andy McCluskey and later took great delight in recounting the story of how he'd bowled him out during a cricket match between the two bands. OMD, supposedly, were all out for eleven.

The undoubted peak would come with their 101st performance of the tour in front of almost 70,000 people at the Rose Bowl, an enormous American Football stadium, in Pasadena. None of them were sure if they'd ever play a venue that big again and so they decided they needed to record it. With extraordinary ambition they contacted DA Pennebaker, the director who recorded Bob Dylan's legendary "rockumentary", *Don't Look Back*.

They had little idea at that point of what exactly they wanted. They'd developed a fascination with America on their frequent trips to the country and there was some suggestion that they make a road movie. The only problem with that idea was that they didn't actually spend much time on the road anymore. As a rule they flew from city to city. A film of them getting on and off jets didn't sound too exciting but then again they wanted more than just a straightforward portrayal of the show.

"We knew what we wanted to avoid more than what we wanted to get," said Alan. Their next idea was to follow the fans as they made their way by bus to the Rose Bowl. With that end in mind, they invited them to audition for a part in the film at a club in New York. Thousands turned up but initially DA Pennebaker wasn't convinced that it was going to work.

When they'd initially phoned Pennebaker he had no idea who they were. Nor did he particularly care about their music. He said later that he'd never been a fan of Dylan's music before he made *Don't Look Back,* either. The fans of the music, though, he found fascinating. "What I noticed that made me think there was a film here was the extraordinary relationship I could see between a bunch of well-to-do middle-class American kids and a group of working-class Brits with whom they had almost nothing in common," he said to the *New York Times.* "There was just this abstract, devotional need."

While DA Pennebaker prepared to make the film, the band had the twin anxieties of preparing for the biggest gig of their careers and knowing that it was going to be recorded for posterity. Initially the main concern was whether they could really sell 70,000 tickets. It would be pretty embarrassing to go out there to a half-empty stadium. Their agents wouldn't have suggested the Rose Bowl if they weren't confident that they could at least come close to filling it but there was always an element of doubt. They were particularly concerned because they'd be playing on a holiday weekend when many people would be going away. The film includes footage of their agent anxiously asking if it might be possible to move the stage forward if not enough tickets are sold.

That concern quickly evaporated as the tickets for the whole tour were eagerly snapped up. They announced the Rose Bowl gig at a special press conference on the pitch and it was a rather low-key affair. They arrived in a convertible Cadillac and Dave managed a certain swagger as they strode up to deliver a prepared speech but when they spoke they still came across as the polite, provincial kids that they were at heart. Alan looked rather tired while Martin lurked in the background and Dave smiled behind his shades and did his best to supply the charm quotient for the whole band. They seemed very different to most bands who could fill a venue of this size.

It didn't help that the press didn't seem to realise there would be a Q&A session afterwards so there was an awkward pause when the compere called for questions. Everybody seemed bemused by the event's strangely low-key tone. Pennebaker and his crew were equally unsure of what exactly it was they were capturing. At least they had started to bond with the band, though. It took a while because Depeche Mode were always a little cautious of people they didn't know.

One mooted title for the film was *Mass*. This was obviously a reference to *Music For The Masses* but it was also a reference to the quasi-religious feelings that their most devoted fans had.

Another angle that the film-makers took was that of the 'Master And Servant'. The concept of the song had been taken in many ways by many different people but, intriguingly, Pennebaker saw it as a reference to the relationship between band and fans and band and label. Except, he said, "the roles switch constantly".

Despite allowing the film crew backstage and on the road, the band were careful not to show them too much. Depeche Mode tours at that time could be fairly decadent places. "We never really allowed Don Pennebaker to see the darker side of being on the road," Alan said later.

What Pennebaker captured so brilliantly was the sheer energy of the show. The performance was a triumph. It set the tone for future Depeche Mode stadium shows, not least because so many people saw Pennebaker's film and imitated the behaviour. The orchestrated arm-waving that Dave liked to instigate became a kind of trademark. Even those who liked the band were sometimes alarmed by the power that he seemed to have over thousands of people. Some harsh critics in the media even drew false, alarming, unwelcome and unwarrantied parallels with the Nuremberg rally in Nazi Germany – something the band would find abhorrent. This was partly because of Martin's affection for Berlin but the suggestion was completely against the band's beliefs and besides, the crowds at Depeche Mode's shows were merely being welcomed into having a good time, not into taking over the world. When Dave saw the sea of people out there, it was a moving experience. He was blinking back tears as the crowd sang the chorus of 'Everything Counts' and he admitted in the *101* film that he cried.

Depeche Mode perhaps ended up playing more shows than they were physically, emotionally and mentally capable of dealing with. The $101^{st}$ show was one of those experiences that made being in Depeche Mode worthwhile but it also created an increasingly unbridgeable gap between the way they felt onstage and they way they felt off. Dave, as the centre of everybody's attention, felt it much more strongly than the rest of them. In one interview later he was asked how he dealt with the difference and his glib answer seems very sad in retrospect. "Wouldn't you like to know?" he laughed.

In the same interview he admitted that the whole band struggled to cope with the emotions. There was a build-up of energy on-stage and if they weren't dealing with it through various individual choices of drink or drugs, it came out in other, perhaps equally dangerous ways. In the *101* film, Dave famously discusses his altercation with a taxi driver on that tour. Apparently the driver had alarmed him by driving at dangerous speeds and refusing to slow down. It's a funny story, culminating with the supposedly enormous driver's trousers falling down but it did have a more serious side. He admitted that at that point he'd been looking for a fight for several days. Such a pent-up emotion in a band is a potentially explosive issue, something Dave acknowledged himself in interviews at the time.

Unfortunately there wasn't always a convenient cab driver for them to take their frustrations out on. If there were altercations on tour, they were always most likely to be within the band simply because they were in such close proximity to one another for so long.

"When you come off-stage the tension is very high," Dave said in another TV interview. "You're on an emotional high but also you can get at each other. A couple of members of the band have come to blows just because someone's not playing their part properly. And it's so extreme and you're so hyped up and you come off-stage, and basically anyone gets it if they're in the way. And a couple of times there've been fights – actually real – they've been broken up and we've had to go back onstage to do an encore." This genuinely happened on the *Music For The Masses* tour. Fletch and Alan came to blows in Salt Lake City and then had to go back on to play the ultra-chirpy 'Just Can't Get Enough'.

Peter Care, who directed three Depeche Mode videos in the mid-1980s, says that he understood what was happening to Dave with his increasing drug abuse and that it was certainly not atypical of musicians in his position. It was a way of coping with the extraordinary emotion without blowing his top. "I always feel sympathetic for singers like him," he says, "because I don't know how you come down off the high of singing to 50,000 people or whatever it is. How do you deal with the boredom of waiting around? I don't understand how all singers aren't addicts! It's amazing to me how they can keep sane."

# 11

# VIOLATOR

After Pasadena there was a feeling that, surely, Depeche Mode must have peaked. Even people who'd criticised them in the past were starting to come round to the idea that to play electronic music in venues this big meant they must be doing something right. There were no other "synth bands" on anything like the same level. Most of their contemporaries had long since fallen away.

"Against all odds, there's something terribly charming about Depeche Mode's penchant for dubious visual imagery, equally dubious leatheriness and a set of songs ostensibly about sex in all its glorious permutations," said *Record Mirror* of their Wembley show in 1988. That year alone they played to nearly half a million Americans; without selling vastly more records, they were vastly more popular.

When Dave got back to Basildon, it was inevitably difficult to adjust. It didn't help that the problems with obsessive fans had gone from bad to worse. One of them actually hired a private detective to follow him home from the studio and find out where he lived.

"I lost my rag and really shouted at him. I told him, basically to fuck off," he told *Rolling Stone*. "Later I sent the guy a letter saying, 'I apologise, but you must respect my privacy. I want to have some time with my wife and son.' He sent back a letter saying, 'I'm sorry I bothered you, and I won't ever do it again.' Then, right at the end of the letter, he said, 'By the way, would it be possible for me to come round next weekend?' I just thought, 'Well, that's it. It's time to move.'"

Part of the reason for their success was that electronic music was suddenly fashionable again. Without having to change direction at all, suddenly it seemed like everybody else was heading their way. The year 1988 was dubbed the 'Second Summer of Love' as Acid House took off and raves started sprouting like magic mushrooms in the British countryside.

Depeche Mode took as little interest in this phenomenon as they

Early Depeche Mode shot: Andrew Fletcher, Dave Gahan,
Martin Gore, Vince Clark.
*Harry Goodwin/Rex Features*

Dave's suit phase, Nottingham, November, 1981.
*Andre Csillag/Rex Features*

The leather look on display in the early 1980s.
*Phil Loftus/Retna*

Dave and Martin Gore in the mid-1980s.
*Ian Hooton/Retna*

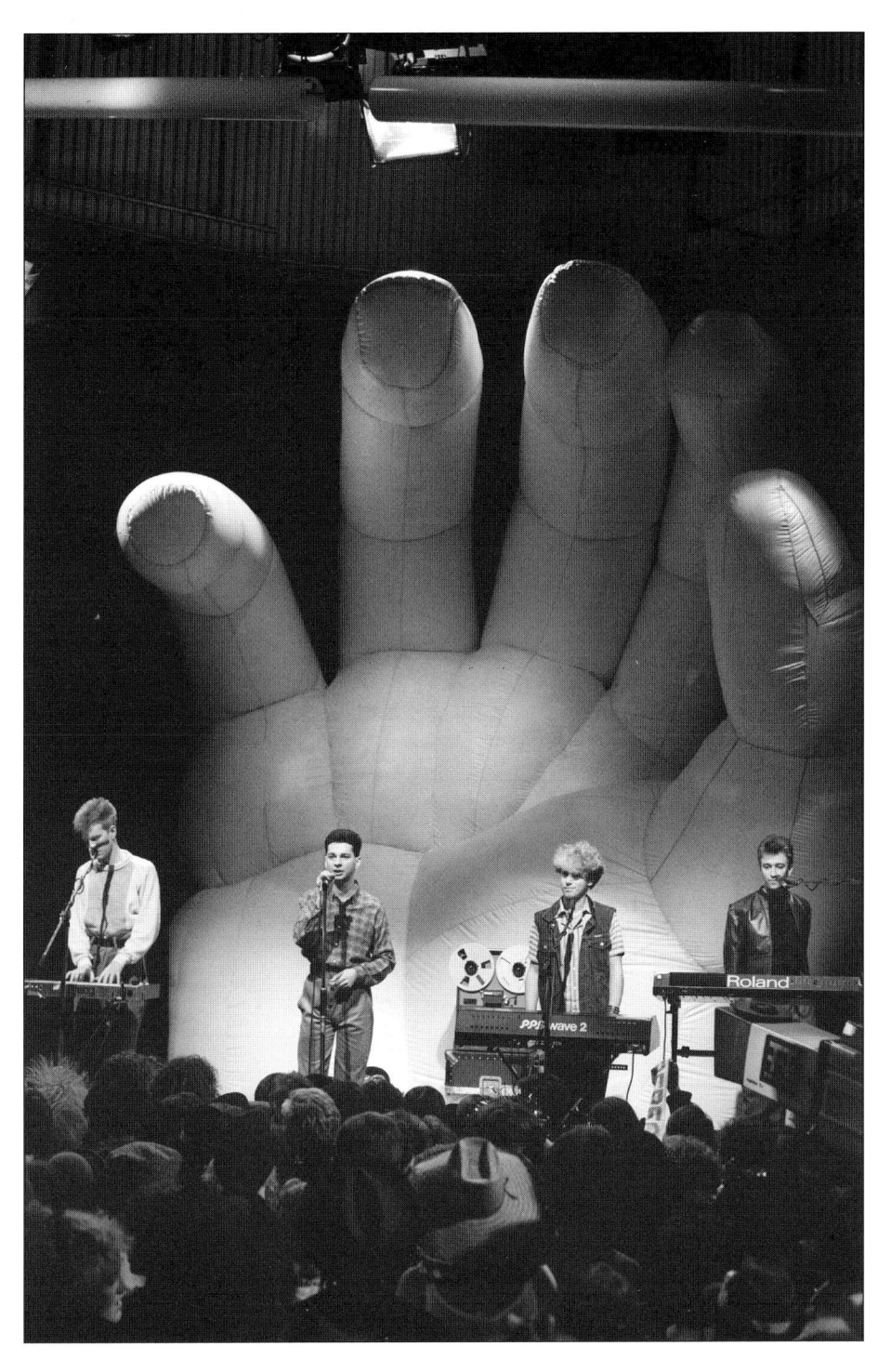

An early Depeche Mode TV performance on *The Tube*, 1983.
*ITV/Rex Features*

Depeche Mode: Andrew Fletcher, Alan Wilder, Dave Gahan, Martin Gore.
*Andre Csillag/Rex Features*

Montreux Pop Festival, Switzerland, 1987.
*Brendan Beirne/Rex Features*

Dave and Andy relax at the Pasadena Rose Bowl, June, 1988.
*Adrian Boot/Retna Pictures*

Live at Earls Court, London, January, 1993.
*Mick Hutson/Redferns/Getty*

Dave and Martin performing at Wembley Arena, October 18, 2001.
*Jim Dyson/Getty Images*

Recording at the Electric Lady Studios in New York, March 14, 2003.
*Cody Smyth/Retna*

Depeche Mode in concert, Wembley Arena, April 3, 2006.
*Brian Rasic/Rex Features*

Performing live on TV in Salzburg, Austria, January 28, 2006.
*Action Press/Rex Features*

Dave and Jennifer at the *Control* film premiere, New York, September, 2007.
*Sylvain Gaboury/Rex Features*

Depeche Mode live at the Echo Music Awards in Berlin, February 2009.
*Axel Schmidt/AFP/Getty Images*

had all the other scenes and movements that had come and gone during their career. At the end of 1988, though, after three other singles were released from *Music For The Masses* ('Never Let Me Down Again', 'Behind The Wheel' and 'Little 15'), they allowed ultra-hip Bomb The Bass musician and producer Tim Simenon to do a remix of 'Strangelove'. They hadn't been totally happy with the original single version and they'd re-recorded it for the album but the remix tied them neatly into a dance scene that was now starting to acknowledge their influence.

In February 1989, style magazine *The Face* put them on the cover asking whether they were the Godfathers of House music. It was a dramatic turn-around from the way they'd been seen for the last eight or nine years. The band were bemused by the attention, having little or no interest in the club music of the time. Nevertheless when the magazine took them out to Detroit to meet the likes of legendary techno pioneer Derrick May, they were gratified by the attention. He took them to the famous Music Institute, the club that was then at the heart of Detroit's techno scene and they were astonished that people knew who they were. "We weren't getting much attention at home so to be mobbed by black kids in Detroit is something," Fletch said. "We thought we must be doing something right."

Despite the success of *Music For The Masses*, they thought it was time to do things differently. Martin, in particular, was conscious of the dramatic gap between the size of their live shows and the number of people who bought their records. They were playing the same stadiums as bands like Fleetwood Mac and Bon Jovi who sold twenty times as many records.

Also, they were bored. Previous albums had involved intensive pre-production and planning. They had a formula that had become extremely successful. It was a way of working that had started to feel stilted. "We wanted the songs to come across in a more direct way and not to be so fussy and critical about things," said Dave in a TV interview. "We wanted to try and get a lot of energy on tape when we're recording, rather than play around with sounds for so long until by the time you go to record it you've forgotten about the direction of the song."

It was an oblique criticism of the way they'd worked in the past.

Much later on, Dave would talk about feeling frustrated and excluded in the studio because his contribution was often limited to singing. In 1989, though, they all wanted to do something very different for the new decade. "We decided that our first record of the 1990s ought to be different," Martin said. "We knew it was bound to still be Depeche Mode because my writing style is so characteristic and inherent to the songs."

This meant, among other things, a change of producer. Their initial choice was Brian Eno. The former Roxy Music man was known as one of the world's most innovative, unusual musicians but he'd also co-produced enormous selling albums like U2's *The Joshua Tree*. Instead though, they chose somebody who'd worked heavily with Eno: Flood, his engineer on *The Joshua Tree*. Flood had made his name working with many of the coolest acts of the electronic avant-garde in the early 1980s, including Cabaret Voltaire, Soft Cell and Psychic TV. It was quite a turn-a-round for him to be working with Depeche Mode, formerly considered the gawky pop puppies of the electronic litter.

They weren't yet in the same league, commercially, as U2 but they would be the biggest selling band he'd produced on his own. It was a big responsibility because they still craved a headmaster figure, somebody with a casting vote when the band's precarious democracy meant they couldn't agree. This was something that Flood excelled at. He was good at tactfully suggesting a change of direction without getting people's backs up. He didn't have the ego of some so-called "super-producers" but he had a knack of getting the best out of bands without imposing his own personality on the record. There was no specific 'Flood sound' and yet he was capable of doing far, far more than just an engineering job.

In May 1989 they went with Flood into Logic studio in Milan. They didn't get much done to start with, but only because of the new restrictions they'd set themselves. They'd wanted to be more spontaneous but this often meant trying things out and having to abandon them. It was a fun period when anything seemed possible. They left behind some of their previous ways of working, guitars were more in evidence and they jammed in a way that they hadn't done before. Dave was there far more often than he'd been in some previous sessions. Often in the past he'd only really felt part of things when it was time to perform his vocals. This time it was a little more like the band vibe that he was looking for.

"In the past I'd always demo-ed the songs at home and presented them to the band in quite finished form," Martin said to *Select*. "By that stage your ideas are pretty fixed, so we had tended simply to copy the demos, to make them better. But this time the band asked me to keep the songs as basic as I could."

This meant they had to work on them in the studio, trying out new things and recording the same songs over and over. In the early part of their career, this would have been cripplingly expensive. They simply couldn't afford to use valuable studio time playing around with ideas. They needed to work out what they were going to do in advance. The financial success of the *Music For The Masses* tour, though, had given them a new freedom. One example was 'Enjoy The Silence'. It started life as one of Martin's slow ballads until Alan suggested speeding it up. When they added the guitar riff it became something very different to what they'd originally intended. "It's the first time ever in our whole career that we've actually thought we've got a hit single," says Fletch. "We just knew straight away."

With other tracks the approach had the opposite result. They tried recording 'Policy Of Truth' numerous different ways before finally settling on something that was close to what they'd had in the first place. Surprisingly Martin felt that it sounded too much like their previous records.

"'Policy Of Truth' we recorded several times in different directions and it just didn't work," said Martin. "A lot of the songs were like that. So by supposedly being more spontaneous we ended up spending more time in the studio."

After Italy they headed off to Puk in Denmark where, after the work-hard, play-hard vibe of Milan, things became more intense. They chose Puk partly because it was so isolated in the Danish countryside. The nearest town was fifteen minutes away and there weren't any distractions. There was nothing to do but work. It wasn't easy but it was becoming clear that this would be their best album yet. Dave's voice was far more restrained and mature than in the past, helped by the fact that Martin's lyrics had drastically improved. He was still writing about the same themes: religion, sex, guilt – but there were fewer forced rhymes and a greater subtlety.

There were also early warnings of the dark side of their "partying" with 'Sweetest Perfection' and its reference to the "thug" that could be brought out by drug abuse. On another track with a similar theme, 'Clean', Dave's voice is thick with bitter sarcasm as he claims to have changed his routine. Of course he'd only recently got into a routine that was very far from "clean" and it would last for some time to come.

At the time, though, Fletch was more of a worry and in the end they suggested he go back to London and he duly checked himself into a clinic for stress-related issues. Meanwhile, the rest of the band were finishing the record with Flood and mixer Francois Kevorkian. Francois was best known for his work with Kraftwerk and he came from a dance background that was very different from Dave, Martin and Alan's. Although born in France, he made his name as a DJ on New York's vibrant disco scene in the late 1970s. The meeting between the band and Francois was something of a culture clash. He was loud and exuberant. They never quite knew what reaction they were going to get from him. Often he would work long into the night, obsessively tweaking the sounds to try and get them right.

With Kevorkian on-board as a mixer, it might have seemed logical to exploit their new status as supposed dance überlords but the songs Martin had written weren't four-to-the-floor dance tracks. The first one that they gave him to remix, 'Personal Jesus', was still an electronic track but it had a bluesy, twangy feel. It had – shock of shocks – a guitar on it. It wasn't the first time they'd used guitars, there was a distorted guitar sound as far back as *A Broken Frame* but never as prominent as this. They naturally wondered what their fans would think.

"We thought that especially in America, it might struggle for airplay and things like that," said Martin, "and we were proven totally wrong."

It was also the latest in a line of songs where they'd utilised the percussive qualities of their packing cases. They recorded two or three people jumping up and down on them and then sampled and looped the sound as the beat. The track then, had a thudding, organic quality that was unlike anything they'd done before and yet it was a natural progression in their experimentation with sounds.

## DEPECHE MODE & THE SECOND COMING

They released 'Personal Jesus' while they were in the studio making *Violator*, and, although it wasn't picked up by radio in America straight away, it was played in clubs and became a word of mouth phenomenon. It would take six months to go into the US Top 30.

"It sold half a million records before it started being played on the big radio stations," said Martin to *Melody Maker* at the time. "It just built up in the clubs for five months and the radio ignored it. Most of them still aren't playing it. Too weird mate! Too f***ing weird! They just don't get it."

The song hung around for so long that many alternative stations in the States started playing the b-side 'Dangerous' and that also ended up charting on radio play alone. They'd worried that they might have problems with religious groups crying 'blasphemy' but in fact many Christians were able to interpret it as a genuine ode to Jesus. Years later when Johnny Cash covered the song, that was the element that he drew upon. The adverts for the single, a phone number with the simple legend 'Your own personal Jesus' caused more furore. They were rejected outright by some regional newspapers and *The Evening Standard* in London raised objections, before eventually relenting. Martin admitted, later, that they might have had a point. In fact, Martin revealed later, the song was inspired by a book Priscilla Presley wrote about Elvis.

The single was helped on its way in America by a video from Anton Corbijn that with its cowboy imagery dramatically took them away from their European image. It featured them in a Western style bordello, a cheeky nod to their new status as one of the few British bands to become big in the States at that point. To make it they flew out to a desert in southern Spain where many of the classic Spaghetti Westerns had been filmed. Dave particularly enjoyed winding up Andy by telling him that they were going to have to ride horses. In reality it was a rocking horse. "It spoiled my whole day thinking about that," he complained afterwards.

Even without the video, though, 'Personal Jesus' would have struck a chord with millions. The twanging guitar and striking vocals were simultaneously resonant and intimate. It was arguably only the second Depeche Mode song, after 'Just Can't Get Enough', to reach out beyond the usual record-buying public and become a part of the culture. It was ultimately a massive hit all over the world and became the top selling twelve-inch that Warner Brothers had ever released.

When they chose it as a single, Flood described it as "the perfect track to say 'Here's Depeche Mode, but not as you know them.'" They were fortunate that they had such a distinctive sound, not least with Dave's voice, that they were able to change direction dramatically and still sound distinctively Depeche Mode. The band had indisputably changed but not just musically.

Dave's years of craving domesticity and stability were over. The success of the *Music For The Masses* tour had changed him and the rest of the band noticed the strain starting to tell. His appetite for partying was becoming a problem and he told the media he sometimes felt an unease every time he went home to his wife and son.

"It began during the making of *Violator*," he said to *Mojo*, "when I was doubting that marriage was for me. You know, the big house in the country with a couple of cars in the drive and a dog running round. Playing happy families, in between this thing … this Depeche Mode thing. I felt fraudulent in that situation. I was scared and the best thing I could think of was to run away."

Martin and Fletch weren't always sympathetic. Fletch said that he just tried to avoid the singer whenever he could. As musicians they were approaching an astonishing peak but as people they were fragmenting. Still, at least the record provided some consolation. Dave knew they'd done something exceptional. When they were promoting *Violator*, Martin cautiously hedged his bets, saying that bands lose all perspective on albums by the time they've finished them. "You're too close to it until it's actually out," he admitted in 1993. "I wasn't sure I even liked it until a year or so after it was out." The singer, though, was predictably more gung-ho. He was able to say categorically that this was the best record they'd ever made.

There aren't many bands around whose most acclaimed album is their seventh.

## 12

# WORLD VIOLATION

When the new album was released on March 20, 1990, it received some of the best reviews of the band's career. As Dave said later, many of them were variations on: "I hate this band but this album's great." Only *Rolling Stone*, never fans, held out from the consensus, opining: "It's becoming increasingly clear that the group will never again make a number as compelling as the 1981 gleeful rubber-duckie disco tune 'Just Can't Get Enough.'"

*Violator* is now regarded by many people as Depeche Mode's best album. For a record that was, at times, such a struggle to make, it sounds remarkably unforced. It has a smooth, slick sound with none of the hectoring quality of some of their early tunes. Instead Dave's voice rides the wave of the music almost laconically. Compared with the other alternative dance music that was around at the time, it's noticeably restrained and mature. They sound like the elder statesmen of pop that they were by then and yet Martin hadn't lost his knack for writing great tunes. They were catchy but they held something back which made it an album – unlike many pop records – that was difficult to tire of. It was hugely influential on bands ranging from the Pet Shop Boys (who said that it had "raised the bar") to later industrial acts like Nine Inch Nails.

When Dave left for the *World Violation* tour, it felt like he was stepping back into his element. He wasn't always comfortable at home anymore but on stage he was the undisputed master of all he surveyed. The rest of the band gladly let him take control in a way that was unthinkable in the studio. They understood that this was what he was born to do. On stage they all felt invincible but this exacerbated the predilection for excess; by now they felt like they could do anything. They'd become, almost by stealth, one of the biggest bands in the world.

This was vividly illustrated by one incident before they even played their first gig of the tour. During a previous year's radio interview with the KROQ radio station in LA, the DJ, ex-pat Englishman Richard Blade, had drawn a promise from them that they'd come out and do a signing session the next time they were over. They readily agreed but when he talked about the 60,000-plus fans who'd attended their Rose Bowl concert, they jokingly pointed out that they weren't about to sign 60,000 record sleeves.

It was a joke that came perilously close to the truth. In conjunction with KROQ they arranged a session at the Wherehouse Record Store in Beverley, Los Angeles. They had no idea how many people would show up but there was always a slight fear with these kind of things that it might be embarrassingly few. A few hundred would be fine but any less than that could make them feel a bit foolish, any more would turn into a gruelling day's work.

However, when they arrived, they heard there were already queues stretching around the block outside. Then, while taking part in a radio interview for KROQ, they heard reports that 10,000 people were waiting outside and then 15,000. Eventually police had to be called because the shop's security guards couldn't control it anymore. It was fantastic publicity but for a while they were terrified that there could be a real disaster. At one point the windows were actually bulging inwards as people pressed against them. Eventually the police announced that they had to cancel the signing. The band went back to their hotel, switched on the news and saw they were one of the main items, with some fans supposedly rioting when they found out about the cancellation.

"It actually got quite scary," said Dave. "The whole thing got a little bit out of control. There was no way we could have known that there was going to be so many people turn up … you could feel the atmosphere in the place building up. We just all kind of looked at each other and said, 'We gotta get out of here!'"

Although one woman was taken to hospital after being caught in the crush, they were relieved to hear that nobody was seriously hurt. Nevertheless Depeche Mode called a press conference afterwards to apologise and to subtly play down what had happened. When a reporter asked them how they felt about the "riot" Dave leaned over to Alan and whispered, "That wasn't a riot, Chelsea on a Saturday afternoon, that's a riot."

# DEPECHE MODE & THE SECOND COMING

*Violator* went on to sell seven million copies, vastly more than any of their previous albums. They thought they'd peaked with *Music For The Masses* so perhaps they weren't ready for the intoxicating heights that they'd now hit. "Till that point, we'd been ticking along nicely, selling well, never too much attention paid to us," said Martin to *Q* in 2005, "then suddenly *Violator* took off. It went over the edge in America. Pressures immediately doubled or tripled."

It all succeeded in creating tremendous anticipation for the *World Violation* tour. It was much bigger than anything they'd done before. The new visual element provided by Anton required a much bigger crew as well. They ended up travelling with eleven articulated lorries and almost 100 roadies, engineers and technical staff.

They started out in the heat of Pensacola in Florida. It was in a part of the state rather unfairly dubbed "the redneck Riviera", hardly classic Depeche Mode territory. They'd never even played in Florida before and when they arrived portents weren't great. When they went outside the Civic Center where they were due to play they were frequently greeted by truck drivers leaning out of their windows to shout "faggots" at them.

"This is a sort of backward place, isn't it?" Alan Wilder complained to *Rolling Stone*. But, despite this, the Civic Center had sold out. They'd sold upwards of 18,000 tickets for stadiums in Texas and Kansas, too – other states where they didn't receive a great deal of radio play. In New York they sold out 42,000 tickets for the Giants Stadium in a day. By then *Violator* had already sold more than a million copies in the States. It was the kind of success that bred more success. The bigger they got, the more inclined the radio stations were to play them. So then they got bigger …

Dave would later recall it as the last tour where the "partying" was genuinely fun. His drug consumption escalated. With their new status as a genuinely big band they were treated like kings in every town they visited. After virtually every gig they'd go out on the town and club owners would fall over themselves to give them the best hospitality.

"We hit a point during the *Violator* tour where everything was just great," Dave said to *Q*'s Dorian Lynskey in 2001. "But I think I overdid it even then. Every night, after coming off stage, we'd all get on one and go out … if you can imagine going out on tour for a year and a half and you're like this circus and then you finish all that and come back to the reality of your life. The longer those tours got, the less satisfied I became with normal life."

In retrospect their later *Faith And Devotion* tour would become legendary for its debauchery but the *World Violation* tour wasn't much better. It was the start of Dave's darkest period as his drug abuse moved to a heavier level and he went back to the heroin that he hadn't touched since his teens. "It was an escape," he said to *The Times Magazine*, "heroin meant that I didn't have to deal with my feelings of being an outsider, an oddball. With heroin I didn't have to deal with anything." Disastrously he got the impression that he could run away from normal life and disappear permanently into a world of sex, drugs and rock 'n' roll.

He also had a new love in his life, a lady who was working within music PR. "I was in lust," he said of Teresa in *FHM*. "I cut off everyone who had ever been involved with my life up to that point. I started anew." On the *World Violation* tour, the cracks in his well-being started to emerge but he wasn't yet beyond the point of no return. It was, significantly, a lot shorter than the major tours on either side of it and it just seemed on the surface like they were having fun.

"There was a lot of ecstasy around, but I couldn't say that anybody was adversely affected by that," said Alan Wilder to Stephen Dalton in *Uncut*. "Apparently, Dave was using heroin, but this wasn't obvious in his performances, and there was the usual amount of drinking and frivolity. It was a long tour and maybe there was a delayed reaction, with the cracks appearing later."

But there were ominous signs on the first night. They brought Electronic along as support, the "supergroup" formed by Bernard Sumner of New Order and Johnny Marr of The Smiths. Their excellent debut album had come out that year and they were the height of cool. At the party afterwards, though, Bernard ended up filling the shower with vomit after indulging in liquid ecstasy.

They'd reduced the length of the tour slightly from the 101 dates on the *Music For The Masses* blockbuster but it would still be 75 gigs, sometimes in stadiums of 30,000 or more people. But if anybody was worried about the band at that point, the quality of the performances assuaged their fears. From the start of the first show in

## DEPECHE MODE & THE SECOND COMING

Florida, in front of a giant "DM" and a barrage of lights, it was the most impressive gig they'd ever staged. They started with the instrumental 'Kaleid' and then Dave ran down to the front of the stage, while the rest of them stayed on the level above. The songs on *Violator*, which sounded relatively low-key and subtle on record, were simply enormous live.

By now Dave knew exactly what he had to do to incite a reaction from the crowd. The rest of the band simply formed a "V" (for *Violator*) behind him and let him get on with it. Alan would know every night exactly where he would be at any given moment because by now Dave had honed his stagecraft to a fine point. It was also a strenuous work-out. As well as the vitamins and other medicines that had come with them on previous tours, he was relying heavily on pain-killers to cope with the jarred knees and strained ligaments. "My legs were always hurting. I was always aching," he said to *FHM*, "so, before a gig, a doctor would show up and painkillers would be prescribed: back pain, this pain, that pain. Later on, there were steroids for my throat. And when you put drink into the mix as well, I was like a garbage can."

The shows were given a further visual boost with two giant screens featuring images selected by Anton Corbijn, often emphasising the band's frequently misunderstood sense of humour. Martin was seen wearing a pair of wings and drifting upwards as what Anton described as the "bondage angel".

The set subtly moved things in more of a dance direction but without losing sight of the fact that the songs came first. 'Behind The Wheel' was given a much more beat-heavy treatment and 'Everything Counts' was also turned into a kind of dark techno. Dave's performance, though, kept things firmly in the rock show tradition. Even during the darkest songs, the frontman would revel in the crowd's attention, whooping at any given opportunity and exercising his trademark spinning-top twirl or leaning backwards with his arms spread wide in a Christ-like pose. The fusion between the two styles was best exemplified by their cover of proto-rock standard 'Route 66'. It was a pounding, dance version that still exuded a pure rock 'n' roll spirit and they closed the set with the song every night.

Afterwards Dave craved the same kind of highs off-stage, too.

There was a massive imbalance in his life between the hour or two onstage in the evening and the rest of the time. "I think he just felt that performing was the only thing he could do right," Fletch said later in *Details*. "He was very emotional with all of us. I personally tended to steer clear of him." He was also becoming a clichéd 'rock star' in some ways. It was as though he was starting to live out a rock star fantasy he'd had as a child back in Basildon. It was a strange contrast to the restrained cool of the music on *Violator*.

"We used to joke about *Spinal Tap*," he said later. "We'd always be playing the video on the tour bus or quoting from it. Then it was no longer funny because I was living that life. Losing my sense of humour almost killed me."

As they went round the world, three more singles were released: 'Enjoy The Silence', 'Policy Of Truth' and 'World In My Eyes'. The second was an even bigger hit than 'Personal Jesus'. It went Top Ten in the UK and the USA and, naturally, to Number 1 in Germany. For the first time in their career, they seemed to be getting everything right at once. Once again they were helped by another great video from Anton Corbijn but, when he explained the concept to them, Dave was initially far from convinced. It's "Dave dressed up as a king, walking around with a deck chair," he said.

"Fletch and Mart and Al were rolling around in fits of laughter," he said in a TV interview later, "because they didn't have to do anything, which is what they really like. But his idea was really vague at that time. I didn't really get it."

The singer initially asked him to come up with a different idea but Anton said later that when he had an idea in his head he found it difficult to change it. They were faced with a choice between doing what he wanted or hiring another director. They chose Anton and, in the end, they were very glad that they did. The rest of the band, as Dave had said, liked the fact, at least, that they didn't have to do a great deal. They merely went to a studio and were filmed hanging around for an hour or so, while their singer, Anton and producer Richard Bell, had to spend six days in various frozen locations in the Alps and then Scotland. "It was quite hard work, but it was a lot of fun," Dave said afterwards. "And I got to dress up as king, with the crown and everything."

It is quite an extraordinary video. There are no special effects.

# DEPECHE MODE & THE SECOND COMING

There's just Dave Gahan wandering around various picture postcard locations with a deckchair under his arm. Part of its brilliance is that it's at once very funny but also strangely sad. Anton said that his idea was of somebody who has everything finding peace in simple things. Dave, though, doesn't seem peaceful as he treks from Scotland to the Alps and back. It seemed to capture a kind of loneliness in his character that was usually hidden by the brash on-stage persona and ready wit.

By the end of it, though, he'd had enough. When they came to shoot the final shot of the king in the distance, walking away, he decided that he'd done his bit. Anton wanted him to walk across the fresh snow so they could track his footprints into the distance but the idea didn't appeal to him. They were five miles up in the Alps. The air was thin, it was freezing cold and he'd been working on the video for weeks. "I thought, 'You know what, Richard?' I took the crown off, I put it on his head, I took the robe off, I put it on him, I said, 'You fucking do it.' And I got in the helicopter, went down and had a cup of hot chocolate in the hotel!" he said.

This was another point when they realised how acutely Anton Corbijn understood their music. "It was one of those videos that perfectly captured the song," Dave said. "Anton looks through his lens and he can capture through his camera what the music does. He gets what we do."

The shows they then played in Europe were even bigger than the ones in America. At a show in Germany they were amused to have a genuine German megastar dancing awkwardly by the side of the stage: tennis player Steffi Graf. By the end of any long tour things would be starting to unravel for the band. It was a very unreal lifestyle. They had people to tell them what to do, it didn't seem to matter how much people indulged in drink and drugs and yet they were the ones who were nominally in charge. They were the ringmasters but they were also the clowns. Anton Corbijn, perhaps deliberately, captured this aspect of their life in a video for 'Halo' that portrayed them as members of a circus. Although 'Halo' wasn't officially a single, it charted in the US on radio-play and the video for it was one of the best that Anton had ever done. It shows Dave as a strongman married to a clown who ends up having an affair with another clown, played by Martin. If their acting skills weren't up to much in their early videos, things seem to have improved here. Like 'Personal Jesus', this too was both funny and sad.

That year, having been largely ignored by the British music industry in the past, they also managed to blag a Brit Award. The 'Best Single' was voted for by listeners to Radio One and viewers of Saturday morning kids' show *Going Live*. Uncontroversially, you would have thought, the Depeche Mode fan-club urged members to vote for 'Enjoy The Silence'. This they did in their thousands, prompting the *News Of The World* to run an outraged article declaring that, "Depeche Mode fans are being urged to spend a fortune to FIX it so their favourite group wins a prestige Brit Award." Nowadays, of course, the majority of bands have dedicated "street teams" of fans mobilised to vote in any poll they can find.

After ten years, Depeche Mode had suddenly broken through to another level. They'd become one of those bands who sell music to people who sometimes don't even like music all that much. *Violator* was a fans' favourite but it was also the kind of record that was bought by people who only buy one or two records a year. It would be another six years before Dave Gahan would come down.

# 13

# ISOLATION

Depeche Mode's timing had been good with *Violator*. It arrived at a point when thousands of American teenagers and others around the world were getting bored of the stale rock scene. Rock 'n' roll itself seemed tired and the Basildon boys seemed to represent something different, something cooler and more modern. By the time they'd finished the *World Violation* tour, though, rock was about to revitalise itself. Grunge was starting to appear on the radar. It was still an underground movement. Its aficionados thought that it was an alternative to mainstream rock, rather than, as it turned out, a replacement for it. It seemed like something very new was in the air in America.

For Dave, going back to his old life in England didn't seem like an option. "I was really bored and really safe," Dave said to *The Times Magazine*. "I felt really safe in my life in England in lots of ways, and I didn't like it. There I was with a loving, caring wife, a new baby, a big house in the country, a couple of cars in the drive, and it just didn't feel right. I wanted to move to California but Joanne didn't want to."

Dave was fascinated by LA but, more importantly, he was also fascinated by Teresa. After the *World Violation* tour he finally made the decision to leave Joanne and Jack and move to Los Angeles. "You look at yourself in the mirror one morning and suddenly everything's very, very different and the whole perspective has suddenly changed," he told *Details* magazine. "Last night wasn't just 'I wanted to get laid' – I didn't want to be that person anymore. Teresa brought out some emotions in me that I hadn't discovered, like love."

Nevertheless he was understandably aware he was at risk of doing a similar thing to Jack that his own father had done to him. "My dad left myself and my sister when we were very young, in a very vulnerable position, and I've done the same thing with my son," he said to *Vox*. "But at the same time I haven't, because I'm determined to make it work." He knew he hadn't treated Joanne well for the last few years and, in his own head at least, he was at last doing the right thing. "Over the years, I think I was a pretty shitty person," he continued. "I didn't like what I saw and what I was creating very much in my own life." He was also keen to point out in *Vox* that Joanne "understands the importance of me seeing him and Jack being able to see me. She's been really good about it."

At the time, his new life in Los Angeles seemed like a fresh start, a chance to be himself. Unfortunately he wasn't really sure who that was. "One of my biggest problems is being a people-pleaser," he has said. "I want the whole world to love me. If people seemed like they weren't having fun, I would try to become the centre of attention."

The kind of life he'd been living, with such extremes of emotion experienced on stage for weeks at a time, made him wonder if he should become the kind of person that the fans thought he was. He had something of an epiphany in 1991 when he joined Teresa on the Lollapalooza tour organised by Jane's Addiction frontman Perry Farrell.

"Jane's were just the most incredible thing I'd seen in a long while," Dave said. "Sometimes they were really shit, and sometimes they were just so mountainous and fantastic." Jane's Addiction never reached the lofty commercial heights that they were expected to. Ultimately, they were more significant for the influence they had on the mushrooming 'grunge' scene and for Perry's martialling of the "alternative nation", as he called it, with Lollapalooza. They turned out to be a kind of John The Baptist figure for another band who would change everything in America – Nirvana. Compared with the UK's indie and dance scenes, this all seemed incredibly exciting. As somebody who was first and foremost a performer, there was far more going on with the new breed of rock bands than there was with static electronic groups standing over keyboards. To begin with, Dave just enjoyed being a 'fan', hanging out backstage and seeing a very different kind of music to that which was happening back home. Having spent most of his musical career either in Basildon or in isolation in Berlin, this was perhaps the first time he'd been at the living centre of a 'scene'.

Gradually, though, he started to dream about what would happen

## DEPECHE MODE & THE SECOND COMING

if Depeche Mode managed to capture some of this new energy that bands like Jane's Addiction in particular had found. It made him remember what he'd loved so much about punk when he first fell head-over-heels in love with live music.

"What I was excited about was there were these four different tornadoes that were all coming together and I hadn't seen that ... since I went to see The Clash when I was like 15," he said in a radio interview. His decision to live out the rock star myth for real was not entirely accidental. He'd read the Rolling Stones biography *The Stones* by Phillip Norman and loved the iconic image of Keith Richards as the beautifully wasted rock casualty.

"I actually consciously thought, *There's no f***ing rock stars out there any more. There's nobody willing to go the whole way to do this. So what's needed? What's missing here? What am I missing? It's one thing singing the songs, but does anybody really mean it?*" he said to *NME*'s Keith Cameron. "So I created a monster. And I made the mistake of thinking that meaning it meant you had to take yourself to the very depths of hell. So I dragged my body through the mud, to show that I could do it."

At the end of 1991, Dave Gahan's father, Len, died. He hadn't seen him for years and he'd never been a big part of his life but it was still inevitably hard to deal with. He moved into Teresa's apartment in LA and went to see scores of bands then, a month before his 30$^{th}$ birthday in April 1992, they got married at an Elvis-themed Las Vegas Chapel. It was very different to his last wedding. He wore a see-through shirt to show off a new tattoo and, before they could say their vows, they had to wait for the Elvis impersonator to finish his set.

"In the end, I had to say, 'Will someone get him the f*** out of here? I want to get married!'" said Dave to *Melody Maker*'s Jennifer Nine. "And so Teresa's mum, Diane, sort of politely said, 'Um, excuse me, Mr Elvis, do you think you could stop now, 'cos I think they want to get married.'"

The US rock scene at the time wasn't exactly the most chaste place for Dave to inhabit. Heroin was like a virus that infested the alt-rock scene of the early 1990s. A whole swathe of stars from Kurt Cobain, Layne Staley of Alice in Chains and Scott Weiland of Stone

Temple Pilots were high profile users. They'd started out under the banner of 'alternative' and in some cases ended up replicating the behaviour of the much-mocked 1980s rock stars who'd come before them. Ironically Dave's closeness to Jane's Addiction, through Teresa, meant that he was well aware of how drugs destroyed creativity just as often as they enhanced it. "I'm serious about Jane's Addiction because I still feel they could have been quite possibly the greatest band in the world," he said, "but they blew it because of dope, or whatever, which is really sad."

The day after his wedding, he notoriously had a piercing known as a "guiche", in the area of skin behind the testicles. He said that he'd originally planned to get a ring but that he wanted something a bit more "special". It was like a rock star's version of the showing off in front of the girlfriend that he might have done as a teenager back in Basildon.

"Supposedly you get more sexual energy from it," he said to *Q* in 2003, "but it was the most painful thing I've ever done. As it was being done I was in stirrups for half an hour with this girl staring at my ass, lining the needle up. I don't think I touched my dick for ages afterwards, I couldn't even sit on a hard chair for six months."

"It's kind of a comfort thing," he elaborated later, "you've seen that when you're a little kid and you've got something, the little piece of cloth that you carry around with you everywhere or your pacifier or whatever? Well, I have my guiche."

Understandably, at the back of his mind was his ex-wife and son: "That was always tormenting me," he said to Stephen Dalton of *Uncut*. "It was like I was walking away from something that really was a part of me and I really wanted to nurture in my life. I guess I felt fucked up over that for a while, and trying to drown the feelings. But I spent more time trying to drown the feelings than actively getting off my ass and doing something, which would have been the right thing to do."

Immediately after the *World Violation* tour, he knew he didn't want to carry on doing the same things with Depeche Mode that they'd been doing for the last ten years. They'd achieved everything they set out to and he was far more inspired by rock than he was by electronic music. In LA some of his drug buddies were telling him that he should form his own band. No chance. "I never for a second thought that," he said. "I was happy with Depeche, I just wanted us to rock a little harder."

And, in 1992, when he received a tape of the demos that Martin had been writing, he was immediately inspired all over again. Although Martin wasn't in any way influenced by the new rock scene, he had started to go further with the kind of bluesy style that was evident on 'Personal Jesus'. The first track Dave heard was 'Condemnation' and it fitted with his new state of mind to an extent that was almost eerie. They hadn't even seen each other for the whole of 1991 but, as so often had happened before, Dave felt a real connection between himself and Martin. It was a connection that, oddly, was most acutely expressed through the music.

"It is weird," Dave said to *Video Pulse* magazine in 1993. "It's really strange. I suppose, when I sing the songs, I feel they're mine. I really get into the words. Martin writes from experience, especially his experiences with the band. And because we spend a lot of time together, you'll experience it as well. So lots of times I feel really close, actually, to Martin's lyrics, and especially the last two albums."

He almost found it difficult to believe that the songwriter hadn't, on some level, had him in mind when he wrote the lyrics. He would say later that singing them, particularly 'Condemnation', helped him cope with his own personal problems. As soon as he got the tape he resolved to go back and make an album with the kind of passion that he'd seen in bands like Jane's Addiction.

# 14

# DEVOTION

For the next Depeche Mode album, there was a consensus in the band that they needed to rediscover the closeness that they'd lost in the last couple of years. With the different members living so far apart, it wasn't like the old days when all but Alan Wilder had been based in Basildon. After the end of the *World Violation* tour, they went for many months without seeing each other. When they contacted Flood about working with them again he suggested that they live together to create a more intense working atmosphere. With some trepidation they agreed.

By then they'd worked in many of the major cities of Europe and wanted something new. Martin and Fletch, in particular, always liked the idea of combining recording a new album with living in a new city. This time they fancied Madrid but there were no suitable studios available. Instead they booked a villa a half-hour drive outside of the capital and brought in their own equipment. In 1992 this wasn't as common a method of recording as it's since become. The concept of the 'mobile studio' had only just arrived because of new developments in technology. They imagined that they'd be able to live together and have far more fun than in some sterile studio environment.

It was something that Dave should have welcomed. Of all of them he was the most sociable and the one who was keenest on the idea that great bands were more than the sum of their parts. He loved the idea of the rock 'n' roll band as the last gang in town, partying together and making great music as two sides of the same coin. In practice it wasn't quite like that.

"In theory, it was a really good idea," said Dave to *Future Music* magazine later, "but we found that our personalities clashed incredibly when living together 24 hours a day, seven days a week. I didn't mind it so much, but Alan detested it and Fletch had a hard time. I think Fletch has a hard time being anywhere but home, in his home environment, with his things, his friends, his family, his restaurant."

The moment Dave walked through the door, the rest of the band realised how much he'd changed. Physically he'd transformed himself. He had long, straggly hair, his face was thin and drawn and he had a whole new set of tattoos. "I'd changed," he admitted later, "but I didn't really understand it until I came face to face with Al and Mart and Fletch. The looks on their faces battered me." "I don't think we'd seen pictures," said Martin to Dorian Lynskey in Q. "It was a real shock to see him with long hair, covered in tattoos, even dressed in different clothes. I think when we first got together in Madrid it became obvious that there wasn't a real feeling of band unity."

Dave was so enthused by his own vision for the new record that it hadn't occurred to him that the rest of the band might not want to go down a 'rock' route. "I went back with this attitude like, 'Yeah! Obviously the rest of the band are going to feel exactly like I do!'" he said in a radio interview, "And you know what? They didn't. They were quite happy with the way it all was, and I wanted to turn it on its head and do something that it wasn't."

Although he wasn't the driving force of the band musically, by sheer force of personality he managed to persuade them to go along with many of his ideas. One of his small victories was in persuading the rest of them that they should have a real live drummer. After a few days of persuasion, Alan finally agreed that he would have a go. He'd never played the drums in a band but, as a gifted natural musician, it wasn't too difficult for him to pick it up. At least it gave Dave an outlet for his energy in the studio. They were missing the kind of drive and direction that they'd had in the past and so to begin with there was a feeling of drift. "I felt totally distanced from the rest of the band, I really didn't want to be there," he said. "Up until that point we always felt like a gang – then suddenly it felt really wrong for the first time."

The rest of the band sometimes found it difficult to be in the same room with Dave. His mood swings and reluctance to understand that they might not be as excited by the new wave of rock as he was caused tension. There were arguments but more often there was just awkward silence. Part of Dave's problem was that he often felt frustrated about expressing himself creatively — although he loved to sing, that wasn't enough. In response he spent much of his time painting. It was a surprise to some of the band and he had to remind them that he'd spent three years at art college. At that point he hadn't painted for years but he was so pleased with what he came up with that he gave it to Teresa. He said at the time that he wanted to do more painting in the future.

"It's been a difficult album at times, there's no doubt about it," said Alan to *Vox*'s Martin Townsend immediately after the release. "The fact that we took a break away from each other, that people went and did things with their own personal lives — had children and moved to different parts of the world — has given us all a different perspective on what the group was and is, and what it means to us all. Coming back together has taken a long time to get used to."

It might have been a good idea for them all to live together but not like this. Their rooms were right next to each other in a row but often they wouldn't see Dave for days. They all had their own ideas about how songs should sound and Martin, in particular, wasn't happy about how things were going. Rather than talking about it, though, he would remain silent. Alan was unhappy that they weren't getting anywhere, Fletch was still suffering from debilitating bouts of illness and Dave was in his own little world.

None of them noticed that Dave was doing heroin.

"Through the making of *Songs Of Faith And Devotion*, I was oblivious to the fact that he was even doing drugs," Martin said to Danny Eccleston of *Mojo* afterwards. "All I knew was we weren't seeing him for days on end. I should have put two and two together but … we were all out partying. Getting in at eight in the morning and getting up for work at 12 or 1, we didn't know what day of the week it was, let alone where Dave was."

For Martin alcohol was an issue. "I just drank too much," he admitted to Dorian Lynskey, "I had a couple of seizures and I was told by doctors that it's when your body goes into withdrawal. So sometimes I woke up after a heavy night, started having a panic attack, then I'd immediately think, *Well, if I go to the pub and have a drink I'll be OK.*"

When Daniel Miller arrived to see how they were getting on, he was shocked at the state they were in. Alan would be in one room practising drum parts, Fletch would be reading and Flood would be working, trying to find sounds for them. This was not the close-knit band of previous albums. It didn't help that, while the others had taken almost a year off, Alan had spent the last year working hard on an album for his acclaimed solo project Recoil. He'd barely had a break from the studio and, although he enjoyed spending time there probably more than anybody else, he often felt undervalued.

The only truly positive and energising thing they had going for them was the songs. They naturally had very different ideas about how they should sound, but many of the songwriter's themes struck a chord with Dave. His major inspirations had always been sex, love and religion and this time the latter appeared to be at the forefront.

"I have this inherent longing to want to believe in something," Martin said to Chris Willman of the *LA Times*, "and if I was pushed – no, I don't even think I'd have to be pushed – I would say that I believe in God. And at the time of 'Blasphemous Rumours' maybe I didn't. And I think that comes out in the songs now."

Dave, too, was looking for some kind of spirituality. "We're trying to lift people to a higher level, to take them somewhere where they can find something spiritual, or whatever you want to call it," he said. "One of the big changes on this album is that there's been a hard collaboration to the end, including structures and arrangements and ideas," he told *Creem*. "It's the first time I feel that I've really kind of slammed myself right on top of Depeche Mode."

To some extent the rest of the band were able to ignore Dave's problems because, when it counted, in the vocal booth, he could still cut it. His voice was much more rough and raw than it had been in the past, but they embraced that. Instead of always going for the most technically perfect take, they tried to capture the soul of his voice. It meant sometimes they'd use one of the first takes, even if was a fraction from perfection in places, to get that cracked, emotional quality. It also meant that, later on, he would look back on them as some of the best vocals he'd ever recorded. He wasn't alone in this opinion, as many critics agreed.

When he sang 'Condemnation' he was particularly happy. Martin's original demo was a gospel track and they wanted to retain that element of rawness and simplicity. They also wanted it to have the kind of organic, band feel that had been missing in the past.

"The idea of that track was to enhance the gospel feel that the song originally had without going into pastiche, and to try to create the effect of it being played in a room, in a space," Alan said to *Keyboard* magazine. "So we began by getting all four members of the group to do one thing each in the same space. Fletcher was bashing a flight case with a pole, Flood and Dave were clapping, I was playing a drum, and Martin was playing an organ ... it was embryonic, but it gave us an idea for a direction."

When Dave came to do the vocal, the resulting clatter proved inspiring. At the back of the studio in Madrid was a garage with one room that was lined with tiles giving it a booming echoey acoustic that was perfect for the song. When he walked back into the control room afterwards, he knew how good the vocal had been and he said that the look on Flood's face confirmed it.

"I had a chat with him after 'Condemnation' and he said that was the best track he'd ever sung in his life," studio assistant Shaun de Feo told the author. "He did a lot of his vocals on a crappy mic, in the control room with the speakers on full and just giving it his best. The vocals weren't very technically engineered, it was just the vibe thing. It was a live performance, a lot of those vocals were live performances. You're talking two or three takes. And you're not talking auto-tune then. It wasn't Pro-Tooled up. This was a band. These guys were a band. That's what they were all about and I think that came across on the album."

"That was the one song where I really sang my heart out," Dave said. "I really felt connected to something. It still totally moves me." Flood opined: "Even though he was on heroin and wasn't there most of the time, every time he went into the studio and did a vocal it was amazing."

But although he might have given everything to his vocal takes, Dave later admitted that, in broader terms, his input to the album was relatively limited. "I'd come in with these sporadic ideas and emotions," he said, "but I wasn't there to follow it through. It was really Alan and Flood sitting there at the desk."

Eventually they had to agree that the experiment of living and working together in Spain hadn't worked. They decided, instead, to go back to their spiritual home of Germany. After a brief break they went to another studio at the Chateau Du Pape residential complex

# DEPECHE MODE & THE SECOND COMING

in Hamburg. There, in some ways, things became easier. They'd done the groundwork and Alan, Martin and Flood were able to move forward rapidly, with Dave providing more superb vocals. Chateau Du Pape was much closer to what they were used to. They needed a professional environment to remind them what it was they were there to do. This was much better for Flood too. He'd experienced the bizarre working methods of Depeche Mode with *Violator* but on this album things appeared even more dysfunctional. They often simply didn't talk to each other. Anton Corbijn once said that if U2 had the most meetings of all the bands he'd worked with, Depeche Mode had the fewest.

"The hardest job of all was probably for Flood, pulling it all together," said Dave to Stephen Dalton. "I think that album virtually destroyed him, too. He's worked with Nick Cave and U2 and everyone, but he said to me afterwards that the darkest album he's ever worked on was *Songs Of Faith And Devotion*."

It was at Hamburg that the band finally discovered Dave was doing heroin after Alan found the paraphernalia of addiction in his room. They were furious, not only with him but with themselves. His behaviour suddenly made sense and they wondered why they hadn't realised before. They told him that he had to sort himself out and for a while things improved. Ultimately though, there was nothing they could do. He was still in the euphoric early stages of drug abuse and perhaps hadn't fully realised the extent of the danger.

"There were a lot of people telling me I needed help," he said to Barry Walters of *Spin*. "But I didn't want to listen. And everyone was in denial to a certain extent. To be honest, Martin, Fletch and Alan were pretty naïve. They thought that I had decided to become more reclusive and become this strange rock star."

Unfortunately his success in the vocal booth only confirmed a misguided belief that he needed to put himself through pain to produce anything worthwhile. He'd wrenched the vocal for 'Condemnation' out of himself in a way that was very different to the almost ironic performances he gave on *Violator*. It was as though he was starting to think that being 'real' meant being raw. That had always been the view of the hoary old blues bands and hackneyed rockers who'd sneered at Depeche Mode in their early days. When

Vince Clarke started the band they were always intended to be the antidote to that way of thinking. Yet it is hard not to empathise – or at least see the origins – for Dave's logic, when his vocals were so amazing.

Bizarrely their former songwriter turned up in Hamburg. His new band Erasure, now pretty successful themselves, were there playing a gig. Depeche Mode were surprised to see that he'd changed too. Martin reported afterwards that he even came for a night out with them, something he'd rarely done when he was actually in the group.

After they moved from Hamburg to finish the album at Olympic Studios in west London, things were starting to come together, musically at least, and the atmosphere had dramatically improved. On one track, 'Judas', they'd made the very unusual decision to bring in another musician, Irish pipes player Steafan Hannigan. It was their biggest break yet from the strictures of electronic music.

"They wanted to have a very experimental sound but with real instruments," Steafan told this author. "They were very keen not to just do it on the synthesiser. They wanted real playing and real feeling and for me to react to the lyrics. So they talked me through the lyrics and through what they were trying to get and where it was going to fit in. They had a detailed plan of where it was going to go into the track."

Steafan confirms that in his opinion Dave seemed to be the dominant personality during the sessions, even if he didn't have hands-on control. "They both had their input but he seemed to be the main guy. Very approachable and very hands-on and friendly."

Although this personal assessment may not have been accurate in the technical sense because he didn't write the songs and wasn't the producer, Dave was the person who'd pushed the hardest for them to bring in more and more "human" elements. It was partly just because it made recording so much more fun, no small point as by now they were on their eighth album.

It's also interesting that, apart from the very innermost circle, nobody around the singer had any idea that he was using hard drugs. If he was still taking heroin during this time, he was controlling it very well. Studio assistant Shaun De Feo says that there wasn't any indication that anything of the sort was going on.

"I heard all the stories about heroin afterwards and supposedly he was on heroin at the time but I can tell you I didn't have a clue," he says. "I didn't know until later and I was so shocked. It certainly didn't come across on those sessions."

Steafan was equally surprised when the truth came out later. "I've been in other environments where it's de rigeur for people to pop out the kit and disappear," he says. "I've never done drugs but I know it goes on. I was shocked when I heard about it. I nearly took it personally because when you've met these people and you know how lovely and how dedicated they are and they really take their craft seriously it is a surprise. It was a clean studio, I will say that."

Things were generally much more harmonious at Olympic. By then they'd successfully found a compromise between the different members' visions and they were all heading in the same direction. After the album was released, Alan said that, despite everything, they had finally overcome their communication problems towards the end of the recording sessions. "It's probably only now, in the last two or three months, that the unity of the group has solidified again," he said. "I think, for a long period this year, there were a lot of disparities between the different members of the group."

Steafan agrees: "They were working very co-operatively. Everything was very positive. There was a real excitement about what they were doing. There was a buzz around the whole thing. It was a very creative experience."

It helped that they were excited about their own individual contributions. Dave, in particular, felt far more moved by the soulful, gospel-inspired vocal parts on *Songs Of Faith And Devotion* than he had by the more restrained tones of *Violator*.

Despite everything that's been said since about *Songs Of Faith And Devotion* and particularly the infamous tour that followed, it's evident that for the people who worked with them at the time, their dedication to the music was far more in evidence than any apparent debauchery.

"I've worked with a few of those 'rock star' guys and they were not like rock stars," says Steafan. "It felt a bit like I was meeting a band who'd made a first album and were doing their second album and were going to make it even better than their first. They were not confident that they were making the best album ever but they were confident that what they were going to do was make a statement. I've worked with a few people who were exceptionally rude to the people who worked at the studio but I had none of that with Depeche Mode. There was just this courtesy, which was lovely. They had faith in the ability of people like Flood, like me, like the sound engineer."

Underneath, though, there was inevitably a certain level of pressure. They spent an enormous amount of money recording *Songs Of Faith And Devotion*. After Spain and Germany they'd now booked out the very expensive Studio Two and Studio Three of Olympic for weeks. "Oh my God, their budget must have been horrendous for that album," says Shaun de Feo.

"Those guys worked their butts off big time. Martin would be [there] in the morning, Dave would come in about midday and Alan Wilder would be there. Then Martin, Dave and Fletch would go and we'd be there till five o'clock in the morning. Me, Flood, Chris [engineer Chris Dickie] and Alan Wilder, programming and doing all the stuff. We'd be there till five and then we'd come back in at eleven. It was a hard slog. We'd have to get in fairly early because Dave would want to do a vocal about midday so we'd have to prepare for that, so we'd be in about ten/half ten and then, when that was all finished, something else would happen. Then from about midnight Flood and Alan would do all their wizardry on all the sounds and stuff."

The result was an album that was startlingly abrasive after the slick *Violator*. With the opening screech of 'I Feel You' it almost belligerently announced the change of direction that Dave had been calling for. The riff, too, was the most 'rock' thing they'd ever come up with. There's more to it, though, than just the grungier Depeche that he'd wanted. Equally noticeable are the soul and gospel influences that they'd been absorbing. 'Condemnation', 'Mercy In You' and 'Judas' were all overtly spiritual in their themes; 'Get Right With Me' is gospel-influenced; and even the romantic 'In Your Room' has a kind of celestial choir backing up the singer's melancholic reflections on lust.

They also brought in a string section for the first time on 'One Caress'. As so many bands did in the 1990s they hired Wil Malone,

## DEPECHE MODE & THE SECOND COMING

who'd arranged the strings for Massive Attack's 'Unfinished Sympathy' and he conducted a 28-strong ensemble of musicians in the studio at Olympic. Martin then sang the vocal live with them and, Alan said later, it was the second quickest recording they'd ever done, after 'Somebody'.

But even when they sounded their rockiest, they were still an electronic band. The druggy 'Rush' is harder and heavier than anything on their previous albums but it's still driven by synthetic beats. It's almost like a slower version of what The Prodigy would be doing in two or three years' time. Daniel Miller has made the point that Depeche Mode's version of 'rock' was very different to most guitar bands' versions.

Depeche Mode had simply used the most effective tools they had to make the album. Compared with the brilliant simplicity of *Violator*, the new record could at times seem cluttered and over-cooked. The numerous studios and hours of tweaking with sounds are very audible but there are also some of the band's best moments. Dave's voice is very different than from on *Violator*. Gone is the restrained croon, instead he sounds like he might be singing for the last time. It also shows off his range, emotional and technical, far better than the previous record. From the delicate yet soaring 'One Caress' to the deep, grainy 'Condemnation' there's a huge gap. It's hard to believe it's the same man who delights in spinning like a child on stage. It's not hard to see why it was his favourite album to date.

Afterwards Martin wondered whether they'd done the right thing in going down a rockier root. It was the first time they'd ever calculatedly let themselves be influenced, however obliquely, by what was going on in the wider music scene around them. All of their previous albums had been made in the creative bubble of Depeche Mode. "I think it was always good fun to branch out and do that," he said. "I mean, in some ways we were maybe turning into the band that we were rebelling against when we started out being electronic."

That was certainly the view of some of their fans. Early mentor Rusty Egan remembers being disgusted to see that they had a drummer on stage. "I was so fucking upset," he says. "Why have you got a drummer? Get off the f***ing stage!" If they were turning into a rock band, however, it was more in spirit than sonically. They'd lost that ironic distance that's so characteristic of English bands and inevitably become a little Americanised via Dave's experiences in LA. He was much more earnest and overtly emotional than he'd been back in Basildon. It was a change that had good and bad points but the rest of them sometimes missed the old, fun-loving character they used to know.

"Dave's a brilliant mimic," said Daniel Miller to Danny Eccleston in *Mojo*, "and he used to do this great impersonation of a junkie rock star – kind of based on Mick Jagger in his druggy days. But this time I realised it was for real. His body language, the way he talked – he was just a different person."

The success of the first single to be released from the album, 'I Feel You', probably didn't help the band recover their perspective. Anton's video announced their new direction with tub-thumping directness. It featured Dave, in shades and gangster-style suit, doing his best rock moves, Martin on guitar and Alan on drums. Just to reiterate that this was Depeche Mode as a ballsy rock band, there were also half-dressed girls vamping around them. Watching them play traditional instruments while hearing the song, though, also emphasised how much of their music was still electronic. It felt as though 90% of the song was being played by Fletch, on keys, just occasionally glimpsed in the background. The final shot of Dave undoing his shirt to show off his tattoos was like a challenge to anybody who still saw them as the antidote to the alternative rock scene.

Before the release of the album, the band commissioned Anton Corbijn to film an EPK – an electronic press kit – documenting the making of the record and he began it with a wry kind of caricature of the band that was perhaps very near the truth. DJ and journalist Paul Gambaccinni is seen visiting them all in turn. Fletch is in an office, Alan behind a grand piano playing part of 'One Caress', Dave is slumped on some cushions, surrounded by candles, looking like a hippy and Martin is hiding away in a hotel room with a receptionist protecting his privacy. Humourously it made a very clear point of the distance between them and what different characters they'd become.

Poignantly a rather tired-looking Dave is asked about his

relationship with Martin. "Over the last couple of years I think I've felt a lot closer to Martin," he says. "I've got to know him a lot better. I've liked him a lot more. I'd like to think that he felt the same about me." Much of the film is simply a masterclass in trying not to give too much away. Alan cautiously talks about how much each member of the group has "changed" since their last record. Dave talks about what he and Alan and Fletch bring to Martin's demos.

When 'I Feel You' came out on February 15, 1993, it became the most successful single they'd ever released. The new rockier sound went down particularly well in America, even if the drawn-out screech at the beginning didn't. When they edited that out for radio it soon became ubiquitous on 'modern rock' stations.

After the painfully lengthy recording process, they'd triumphed musically but, as people, they were suffering. They needed a long rest. They'd been recording the album, on and off, from February 1992 to January 1993. It was the longest they'd ever spent on a record. Unfortunately the tour was already booked. These days Depeche Mode was such a huge beast that everything had to be arranged far in advance. Because the recording process dragged on for so long, they had very little opportunity for a break. Alan, in particular, got almost no time off. It was his job to go away and rearrange the songs so they could be played live. Dave, meanwhile, went back into his 'rock star' bubble and prepared for the part of the job that was truly satisfying, the two hours or so on-stage. The rest of the time, though, the fourteen notorious months of the *Devotional* tour would almost destroy him.

# 15

# DESTRUCTION

When *Songs Of Faith And Devotion* was finally released, it was as though Depeche Mode had been gone for an age. Things had completely changed. Grunge had become a formula and its most significant figure, Kurt Cobain, was falling further into his own drug abuse and depression. In the UK, fans were starting to get tired of the seriousness of American rock music and the first signs of the nascent Britpop scene were emerging. As usual, despite their nod towards American rock, Depeche Mode sounded unlike anything else around at the time.

Although it wouldn't go on to sell quite the vast quantities of *Violator*, the new album confirmed that Depeche Mode were still a massive band. *Billboard* magazine later stated that *Songs Of Faith And Devotion* was the first ever 'alternative' album to go straight in at Number 1 in their chart. And, by now, the band had fans in every corner of the world. They were all well aware of the dangers of touring for too long, but equally there was a pressure to play to everybody who wanted to see them. Dave knew how physically draining a long tour could be and he began trying to prepare himself. Despite his continuing drug abuse he embarked on a fitness regime, heading to the gym every day. He would spend three hours doing circuits, as well as martial arts training and time on the fixed bike. He also steeled himself for the tour to come with his most ambitious tattoo yet. He spent ten hours, in two sessions, having wings etched into his back. It was, he said, a Celtic symbol that was supposed to protect against evil. "It was like my wings, really, for the tour," he told *NME* that year. "It was, like, my weapon for the tour – if you can do this, you can do anything, y'know? If you can sit under the needle for ten hours, you can do anything, man."

For two weeks he could barely stretch and when they were rehearsing for the tour it hurt every time he moved. It was as though he felt the need to punish himself. Still the tour was what he'd been waiting for. In the studio he might not always have felt like the most important member of Depeche Mode but on stage he was undoubtedly the focus of everybody's attention. And *Songs Of Faith And Devotion* was designed to be played live. Dave wanted to rock and to experience the acclaim of the crowd, still a more powerful hit than any of the drugs that he used as a replacement.

Logistically the tour was a huge deal. There were 152 people on the road with them, depending on whether you consider the drug dealer to be an official employee or not. There was also a therapist. That had been Alan Wilder's idea. They paid him $4,000 a week to listen to their "ramblings" as he put it.

"The idea was that he could provide some kind of support for those people who wanted it," Alan said to Stephen Dalton in *Uncut*, "although the real reason was to try to persuade Dave to come off smack because we weren't confident he was going to make it to the end of the tour. Ironically, I think everybody went to see the shrink at some point apart from Dave, who was far too wise to the scheme."

Before the tour started the rest of the band had a meeting with the singer. They warned him that if he didn't come off heroin and get clean he wouldn't be able to make it to the end. He agreed but, of course, it wasn't that easy. At that point the press, particularly in Germany, were starting to pick up on the fact that something was wrong but they tried to laugh it off. "They're writing these stories [in Germany] at the moment that Dave has AIDS or he's dying or he's on heavy drugs," said Martin to *i-D*, "and it's so funny because it doesn't actually do us any harm, it sells more records. Anyone reading it must think, *That sounds really interesting, I've got to go and buy that!*"

The tour started at Lille in France on May 19, 1993. They then played on average more than once every two days through to the end of the July before taking a break in August only to give them time to shoot the video for 'Condemnation' with Anton Corbijn in Hungary. To begin with, though, it was the support bands who found things difficult.

Depeche Mode fans were highly partisan and it took something special to get through to an arena of 30,000 or more people who were unlikely to have ever heard their music before. Spiritualized were the first to go, their dreamy gospel-tinged rock withering in the cold atmosphere of sports stadia. It wasn't easy to concentrate with thousands of fans screaming "Depeche Mode" all the way through their set. Then their replacements Miranda Sex Garden found themselves on occasion being pelted with rotten meat and bags of dog shit.

Meanwhile Depeche Mode, with their security blanket of staff, minders and hangers-on had created a kind of weird on-the-road cocoon for themselves. There was a sense of being entirely removed from ordinary life, lost in a world of identikit arenas, airports, aeroplanes and hotels. On the way to shows Dave would travel in one limo, Alan in another and Martin and Fletch in another. At times it was like there were separate, concurrent tours going on.

On many occasions, Dave seemed to have done his best to cut himself off. He had his own dressing room, which he'd decorated with candles and curtains in an homage to Keith Richards, and he would stay there for as long as he could. The divisions between the band members were the worst they'd ever been. Fletch couldn't bear to be in the same room as him, Martin barely tolerated him and even Alan was finding him difficult to cope with. "It wasn't just that they couldn't be with me," Dave said in the EPK for *Ultra* a few years later. "I had problems being with myself."

When the shows were good, Depeche Mode were still awe-inspiring. The adulation of the crowd was becoming more and more important. Their devotion and intensity never ceased to astonish and inspire Dave. At one show in Mannheim, Germany, he got slightly too close to the edge of the stage and realised he was about to fall into the front row. He said afterwards that he tried to think of it as just like jumping off the top of the high diving board when he was a kid back in Basildon. Making the best of it, he plunged forwards and was engulfed by a sea of hands that tore at his skin and his clothes until security pulled him back to safety. It was a terrifying, exhilarating experience to be wanted that badly.

Inevitably perhaps, Dave seemed to have a feeling of invincibility but as the tour went on this was getting harder to sustain. In Hungary his performance wasn't up to his normal standards and he admitted he "felt like shit". His voice stood up remarkably well to the punishment he was giving it but on occasion he was struggling.

# DEPECHE MODE & THE SECOND COMING

Yet despite the demands, somehow he kept on going.

At the band's first London show at Crystal Palace Athletics stadium, the atmosphere was intense and somewhat strange. This time they brought goth-rock band Sisters Of Mercy along with them and, although there were certain similarities between the two acts, Sisters' fans tended to be highly partisan and the two camps didn't get on. It was the goth group's only UK show of the year as well, so many fans came along just to see them. Bizarrely, some left before Depeche Mode even arrived.

By this point Dave was in a bad way. *NME* journalist Gavin Martin interviewed him at Crystal Palace and was shocked at his condition. "His skin is sickly grey, his eyes sunk into bluish sockets. The insides of his long, skinny arms are all bruised and scratched," he reported. Dave claimed that the scratches came from his experiences at Mannheim but there was a part of him that wanted people to see him as the junkie rock star. "I'd take pride in telling you I just shot heroin, y'know?" he said to Chris Roberts in *Uncut*. "Somehow, to me, telling you meant I was being honest. But that's what the drug will do to you – false bravado and strength. You think: *I don't need anyone, fuck you all*."

But in London it was much harder to act like that. His whole family was there, including his son. At the time he said that he was happy that Jack could, at least, see him doing what he did best. "He suddenly realised what Dad does and that I wasn't a complete loser," he said in a 1994 radio interview. "He's got all my moves down and he really enjoyed watching. That made me feel real good."

But inside there were more complicated feelings. Years later he told *The Guardian* that his family were horribly concerned about him. "Finally my brother pulled up the sleeves on my arm, saying, 'What the fuck are you doing to yourself?'" he told journalist Dave Simpson "And I lied. I remember saying, 'It's from when I jump in the audience – I get bruised.'"

One morning he woke up hanging halfway out of a hotel window with people staring up at him from below. He'd obviously stuck his head out to get some air and passed out. If the window hadn't slid down and trapped him in place he could easily have fallen to his death. "I was flabbergasted," he said, "especially once I looked at the time – I'd been there hours."

His state at that point is very clear in the video for 'Condemnation'. Anton Corbijn portrayed him as a sort of wasted messiah. Looking gaunt and woozy in a white vest, he's escorted down a narrow lane by a group of hooded women towards a white-clad bride who looks like she belongs in a shampoo advert. The concern on the faces of the rest of the band, dressed up as monks, might well be genuine. It was Dave's favourite song and so he was bitterly disappointed when the American label said that they didn't want to release it in the States. Instead they had to shoot another video for the American single 'One Caress'. It was a situation that the band frequently found frustrating.

The mid-tour break didn't seem to help much. When they started the tour again, Dave's health deteriorated further. At a show in New Orleans towards the end of 1993, it seemed like his chemical intake had finally caught up with him. "During the last song, all of a sudden I couldn't hear anything but I could see everything, and I knew I was still singing," he said to *FHM*. "It was like I was floating across the stage. I went off and said, 'I can't go back on.' I was passing out." Dave had suffered a small heart-attack; it should have been a warning that he couldn't go on like that.

His doctor told him that if he must carry on with the tour, then he should do it sitting on a stool. Dave bluntly refused to do that. His performance every night was what he was living for. Instead they cancelled the next date, he had one day off and then carried on as normal.

At the end of the year they had another break before heading out again at the start of 1994 for the next leg. It was dubbed the *Exotic Tour*. Such was their popularity now that they were able to play venues across Asia and even Africa that they'd never been to before. It was in some ways a risky prospect. They played in Singapore, for example, a country that retained the death penalty for heroin possession.

Before that they played in South Africa at the most tumultuous period in its modern history, as the National Party was about to release control. The wind of change had finally reached the country. They were building up to their first free elections and, a couple of months afterwards, Nelson Mandela was elected president. "The place was beautiful," said Dave, "but the feeling there was like just before the riots in Los Angeles. We left there and you know the rest. History's been made."

In South Africa Alan finally succumbed to the general walking wounded spirit, after being hospitalised with excruciatingly painful kidney stones. He was immediately rushed to hospital and they had to cancel the next night's show in Durban. Dave and Martin, although disappointed to miss the show, did at least get a break by the sea and a trip to swim with the dolphins. It wasn't to a be a lucky trip for Alan. He also lost about £10,000 worth of clothes in a break-in.

Fletch was ill and keen to point out that the entire fragility of the situation wasn't to be solely blamed on Dave: "You mustn't have this impression that there was one guy having all the problems and causing the whole ship to sink," he said afterwards. "There were many holes in the boat." At the time they just told the press that Fletch had to go home and Alan spent a week teaching Daryl Bamonte his parts.

"He's not been feeling well," Dave told a radio interviewer, "and his wife's about to have their second baby and he's got to sort some stuff out so he won't be doing it. He'll be attending to other things that he's got to attend to."

Daniel Miller was disgusted by what he saw when he went out to see them. Originally they'd been the real life version of his innocent Silicon Teens but the success he'd helped them achieve seemed to have damaged them hugely. "I went out on the tour and thought it was horrible," he said. "I remember being introduced to the official drug dealer and at that point I thought, *Fuck this, there's nothing I can do.*"

In the mid-1990s, self-destruction was very much in the air for rock bands, primarily but not wholly because of heroin. While they were on the South America leg of the tour they heard the news about Kurt Cobain's suicide. Meanwhile Dave had developed a serious obsession with death. At his home in Los Angeles he had a bed shaped like a coffin and on one notorious occasion in Long Island he bit journalist Andrew Perry on the neck and said that he was cursing him. "I remember reading about it afterwards but I don't really remember doing it," he said later. "I think I had some strange fascination at the time with vampires. In all seriousness, I was really starting to move into this place where I really believed what I was creating. I definitely could have been a vampire, in my own head."

Despite this, that night Dave went on-stage and to Andrew Perry's astonishment managed to perform as normal. That was part of the problem. However bad he got, Dave always seemed able to deliver a brilliant show. This just hid the depths of his problems.

When they were offered the opportunity for another leg in America, Fletch was horrified. He was still safely at home in England but he didn't think the rest of them could take anymore. Against their better judgement they went back on the road. By then they didn't know what they'd do with themselves if they went home, anyway.

The singer was very conscious that with so much distance between the members of Depeche Mode, he had nobody to talk to or, euphemistically, to "party" with. He therefore pushed for the notoriously hedonistic Primal Scream to be brought along with them as support. Primal Scream, for their part, said they found it a dispiriting experience, playing to thousands of uncaring fans who were merely waiting for another band. They also said that they'd helped to bring Depeche Mode closer together because, at the time, they'd barely been communicating.

Dave consciously aligned himself more closely with them than he did with his own band. He watched them from the side of the stage most nights and, so he said to *NME* in 1997, helped them out when they wanted drugs.

He also noticed, though, that although Primal Scream had a reputation as one of the most debauched bands in the world, they knew when to stop. They didn't live quite the way the myth suggested. Nobody did. It was a lesson he needed to learn but, by then, he was already too far gone. At the hotels they stayed in, they insisted on not just separate floors for each band member, but a zig-zag pattern so they weren't underneath each other. Just in case one of them decided to have one of their riotous parties. At one such party in Berlin, police were called and a ban from one particular luxury hotel chain resulted. At another in Quebec City, Canada, on September 8, Dave spent the night behind bars after arguing a member of staff but no charges were brought.

## DEPECHE MODE & THE SECOND COMING

It started when they received a memo in French informing them that there would be no power in the rooms between midnight and 5a.m due to works being carried out. Considering how much they were paying for the rooms they were understandably annoyed not to have been informed when they booked. This annoyance increased when they were shown to their rooms in complete darkness.

The Depeche Mode party felt that the staff were being unreasonably rude and obstructive in the circumstances and an argument ensued. When Dave "bumped into one of them", the police were called and he ended up spending the night before their gig in jail. The next day Jonathan Kessler had to turn up and bail him and a member of their security out.

Part of what made the tour tough, besides the unhealthy in-take of drink and drugs, was simply all the travelling. However luxurious the hotels were, it wasn't like being at home and, at times, the flights they took could be downright scary. After the New York gig, on the way to Hampton in Virginia, they got caught up in a hurricane. Initially they tried to make light of it. Martin and Daryl began singing Buddy Holly and Patsy Cline songs (both artists who'd famously died in plane crashes). But as everything went quiet and they drifted into the eye of the storm, they genuinely thought that they were about to die.

"Then BANG!" Darryl Bamonte reported in fan magazine *Bong*. "The turbulence re-started, the prayers re-started (Dave clutching a crucifix!) and our pilots somehow managed to get us down in one piece. However, after spending a night in a hotel in Hampton, we decided that the plane had crashed, we had all died and were now in hell."

The tour paused again but only long enough for them to make the video for the last single to be released from *Songs Of Faith And Devotion*, 'In Your Room'. It wasn't an experience they ever wanted to repeat. Once again they got Anton Corbijn to direct and, when he saw the state of Dave Gahan, he had a horrible feeling that this would be the last video he would ever make for them. In consequence he turned it into a kind of a retrospective or an elegy for the band. It included scenes that referenced many of their earlier videos, including 'I Feel You', 'Walking In My Shoes', 'Halo', 'Enjoy

The Silence', 'Personal Jesus' and 'Condemnation'.

Most sinisterly it featured each member of the band in turn chained to a chair. They'd always relied on Anton to capture the spirit of the band and it should have been a warning that, to outsiders, things didn't look good. Surprisingly, though, on the day of the shoot it was Martin that they were all suddenly concerned about. He spent the whole day in the studio and forgot to eat much more than a sandwich. Immediately afterwards they went out drinking and he ended up having a party in his room at the Sunset Marquis until late. Then, the next day, he remembered that they were due to have one of their rare "band meetings". He managed to make it down but, halfway through, he started having a seizure. He was rolling on the floor and making weird noises. It was a terrifying experience, not just for him but for everybody in the room. "Whenever I see this video, I just think 'Oh, God,' he said later. "It brings back terrible memories."

Ironically Anton's intuition would be proved correct, although not quite in the way that he thought. 'In Your Room' would be the last video to feature that line-up of the band because it was the last video that Alan Wilder would ever appear in.

At yet another hotel, in Denver, Martin was arrested and fined for disturbing the peace after another party. Ironically, they'd been taking it relatively easy. He'd had a loud party the night before but this time there was only a couple of people there.

"They rang me and asked me to turn the music down," he said, "so I did. They rang me again and asked me to turn it down, so I turned it off. Next thing I know there's complete silence and the police knocked on the door. I stupidly opened it. They burst in, threw me on the bed and handcuffed me. There was no music whatsoever playing. I think they were out to get me for the night before." It was as though they were trying to out-do each other with their behaviour. In the end the charges against Dave Gahan were dropped and Martin just got a $50 fine.

The last date of the tour, at the Deer Creek Music Center in Indianapolis, finished with an incident that could stand as a metaphor for the whole fourteen months. At the end of the show, Dave took a running jump and plunged twelve feet into the crowd and smashed into the seats. Security had to go in and haul him out before his injuries were exacerbated by the excited fans. He was stretchered off to hospital again but it was only on the flight out of there, more than a day later, that he felt the pain in his ribs. He later found out that he'd cracked two of them. He seriously needed a rest and he headed off to a ranch in the Sierra Nevada mountains, near Lake Tahoe with Teresa. Unfortunately, while the rest of Depeche Mode were able to recuperate, his addiction was such that there was no respite for him. The band had been together for so long that they were just glad to see the back of each other for a while. They didn't even speak on the phone and they wouldn't play live again for almost three years.

Some of the band have said that the legend of the *Songs Of Faith And Devotion* tour as the most debauched tour of all-time is exaggerated. Martin has said that his own tendency towards excess was worse on the *World Violation* tour. Fletch had his own problems without drugs or alcohol and Dave had been using heroin for quite some time by then. Alan said that it was simply that it went on for longer and was better documented than any tour they'd been on before. The massive success of *Violator* meant they were under more of a microscope than they'd ever been.

Whatever the truth was, Depeche Mode finished the tour in pieces. By the end of it, Dave was even thinner than he'd been when he started, allegedly weighing just over 100 pounds. They all needed healing and domesticity and, to some extent, the rest of them got it. Alan went off into the Scottish Highlands for a holiday with new girlfriend Hepzibah Sessa of Miranda Sex Garden. Martin then married his Texan girlfriend Suzanne Boisvert.

Dave arrived towards the tail-end of the wedding reception with various members of Primal Scream. For him it didn't seem like the tour had stopped.

# 16

# DESOLATION

"For as long as I can remember, I've had this shield between me and life," Dave told Danny Eccleston of *Mojo* in 2005. "As a teenager it was music. Then it was Depeche – that was my identity. Then that identity stopped working and the drugs and booze really kicked in as a new identity. I became so lost I was really unsure whether I could find my way out."

It's odd now to think that he thought Depeche Mode had "stopped working" as an identity. They'd been extremely successful throughout the 1980s and somehow stepped up a level in the 1990s. It's very hard to think of another band who managed the same trick. The answer might be that what Dave looked for in the band, at least as much as the music, was a sense of belonging. It was the gang identity that he missed now that they were so estranged from each other. In the past, although he knew he wasn't as close as Martin and Fletch, he always felt like they were a unit. In 1993, though, the unit was shattered.

Alan Wilder had essentially made the decision to leave at the end of the *Devotional* tour but he knew there was no need to announce it right away. It's well-documented that Alan worked tirelessly in the studio; it is also well-documented about the tensions that arose as a result.

Alan has said that the real problem was with the creative relationship with Martin. Like Dave he found it difficult to guess what the songwriter was thinking. He didn't know whether Martin appreciated the work he was doing or not. Six months after the tour, like Vince before him, he attempted to visit them all and tell them that he was leaving. Characteristically Fletch was cross, Martin was noncommittal, merely shaking his hand and wishing him good luck but Dave, who'd he'd always been closest to in the band, he couldn't get hold of at all.

After his holiday Dave stayed in London for a few months and, without the discipline of singing every night, his heroin habit reached a new level. There were thoughts of wanting to start a family but, as he told *Q* later, "When you're a junkie, you can't shit, piss, come, nothing. Those bodily functions go. You're in this soulless shell."

At last he had some self-awareness but it was too late. When they went back to Los Angeles he occasionally tried to kick the drugs but, however determined he was, it seemed impossible. He checked himself into detox centres but when he came back it was always to find that his friends were still using and he quickly fell back into his old ways. He spent much of his time in a closet on his own, which he dubbed The Blue Room, interested in nothing except the drugs. It had ceased to be a rock 'n' roll thing. It wasn't about "partying" anymore. He just couldn't do without it. Within a few months Teresa had left him. In August 1995 he decided that enough was enough. He checked himself into a detox centre in Arizona and tried to get himself clean.

When he got home, though, it was to find that his house had been methodically ransacked. His Harley Davidson bikes had been stolen and even his cutlery. It wasn't the first time he'd had things stolen either. Too many outsiders knew that they could take advantage of him. "He told me once that people were coming into his house and walking out with TVs and DVDs," says Rusty Egan, "and he was incapable of [stopping] them."

LA was everything he'd wanted but it was eating him alive. If he thought the attention he got from fans in Basildon was extreme, it was even worse now. He even had to get a restraining order out against one fan who started camping outside his house.

None of this helped with his increasing feelings of isolation. He couldn't temper his drug use and, in despair, he checked himself into the Sunset Marquis Hotel. After drinking a bottle of wine and taking valium, Dave phoned his mother. Then he walked into the bathroom and slashed his wrists with a razor.

"I don't think I was trying to kill myself," he told *Uncut* later. "I think again I was just crying out for some kind of attention and really going about it in an odd way, it was a mistake. It was feelings of wanting to disappear – still be here, but just floating around."

He hadn't done enough damage to bleed to death but,

nevertheless, he was lucky that a friend was there and she called 911. That was the one saving grace he had. Later on he reiterated that there were always friends there and that he never intended to kill himself. It was more a way of showing the world how desperate he was and proving to himself that he still had people who would pick him up when he was down. "I feel lucky," he said to MTV later. "I feel very fortunate and grateful and lucky that I've had that in my life."

But of course there was always a risk that he could have died. By the time the ambulance arrived that night, he'd lost a lot of blood and the paramedics were forced to stitch him up there and then without anaesthetic. He passed out and woke up the next morning in hospital. After assessing his condition, he was informed that he'd committed a crime under Californian law by allegedly attempting to kill himself.

But even that didn't shake him out of his torpor. When he was released from hospital he rented a new apartment in Santa Monica and went back to using. He got a rush from everything about the drugs, even the sense of purpose that going out looking to score gave him. He was forced to search for his hit in increasingly dangerous places. That became part of the thrill. Although he'd grown up as a tough working-class kid, he'd never been anywhere like the underbelly of LA's drug culture before. "I've had a few guns pointed at my head and shit like that," he told *Hot Press*.

It was clear to everybody that he was on a downward spiral but there didn't seem to be any way of stopping him. By now heroin had made it almost impossible to live a normal life. He desperately wanted to see his son, Jack, but he knew he wasn't capable of looking after a child so he asked his mother to come out as well. After a futile attempt to lie and pretend that he was taking steroids to help his throat, he was forced to admit that he was an addict. "I looked at my mum's eyes and I said, 'Mum, I'm a junkie, I'm a heroin addict,'" he told *Uncut*. "She said, 'I know, love.' Jack took my hand and led me into his bedroom and knelt me down on the floor and said to me, 'Daddy, I don't want you to be sick any more.'"

For a week over Christmas 1994, he attempted to kick drugs on his own – there was a determination to do so, deep inside – but he knew he wasn't really getting anywhere. For the first time he started attending rehab programmes. "I'd go to these meetings and be fucking high as a kite among all these sober people," he told Keith Cameron. "And you can't imagine a worse place to be when you're loaded!"

Later on, when he talked about the 'Dirty Sticky Floors' single for his first solo album, he would create an almost blackly comic image of his time as a junkie. Apart from going out to score drugs, he spent almost all his time in the apartment with no company except two large Wizard Of Oz statues – the Tin Man and the Cowardly Lion. He used to talk to them and hallucinate that they were talking to him, telling him what a "piece of shit" he was. In a state of terrible paranoia he ended up destroying the Tin Man. He was so paranoid that he was terrified even of stepping out of the door to collect his post. He'd creep out of the door late at night, before grabbing it and rushing back inside.

Much of the time he wasn't able to do anything except watch the weather channel for hours at a time. With more black humour he said later that he was lucky he lived in LA, where there wouldn't be anything more complicated for him to have to hear than the news that it would be sunny everyday.

Eventually, in 1996, he got it together enough to move to New York. It felt like it could be a turning point. Meanwhile Martin had now written enough songs for another album. With some trepidation he called Dave up to suggest they go back into the studio and he was relieved when the singer told him that he was now clean. However they still had the huge problem of Alan Wilder's departure to cope with. It's a tribute to the importance of the keyboard player that Martin decided to replace him with, not just another musician, but, to all intents and purposes, a whole other band: Bomb The Bass.

Bomb The Bass were an electronic band centred around producer and DJ Tim Simenon. In the late 1980s they'd helped propel Acid House into the public consciousness and Tim remained a highly respected figure in dance music. He was also well known to Daniel Miller because he'd been a fan of Depeche Mode since the beginning. Even when he was a DJ he'd been a regular face around the Mute office. When he remixed the 'Strangelove' single he'd also anticipated Depeche Mode's status as unlikely Godfathers of House music. When the two teams met for the first time at Fletch's restaurant in London's Maida Vale, though, both sides were a little nervous. Dave's problems meant he was no longer his old, outgoing self and Martin was never an extrovert. It was left to Fletch to play the host to Tim Simenon, his keyboard player Dave Clayton, engineer Q and programmer Kerry.

"They were really nice," says Dave Clayton now. "I didn't expect them to be that unassuming. Dave is quite an outgoing character but at the time I first met them he was quite introverted because he was, obviously, not well. Martin was quite shy and Fletch they called 'Dad', that was his role in the band!"

At this point in their history, Fletch's importance to the band is perhaps underrated. At that first dinner things went extremely well and not long afterwards they went into London's Eastcote Studios to start thrashing ideas out. It was an extremely productive period. When they came up with the outline for 'Bullet From A Gun', they knew this could work. However, when Dave arrived after the first week, things took a darker turn. It was clear that he was still unwell.

"It wasn't working," says Dave Clayton. "There was a bit of friction, especially between him and Fletch. Between Fletch and Dave and Martin. Fletch was trying to keep it all together. He was the dad. He was trying very hard to get everybody on the straight and narrow. Fletch was fantastic during that period. He spoke to the press ... that's how they work as a team, I think."

However things were difficult for Martin, too. His dad died that year and he was still prone to drinking. It meant that Dave Clayton found he was given a surprising amount of independence and responsibility. "It was quite hard but, because there was four of us, once we'd got used to it and didn't feel embarrassed about it all, it was quite good," he says. "When everything fell down, even if they went on benders we always had things to do. Tim, myself, Kerry and Q would be trying ideas out. At least we were a team and we could keep going, keep working. There was always something we could do. We tried different wacky sounds, we got to experiment. And somehow Martin was still amazingly creative. I've never met anybody quite like him."

At Eastcote they were convinced that the bones of a record were coming together. "Most of the work got done in Eastcote," says

Dave Clayton. "We got all the other musicians to play there, Martin did the guitars there and I arranged the strings for 'Home'. However it was clear that Dave was not really fit to record his vocal parts. They'd mic him up and hope that he could deliver but it was usually no good. It was always Dave that was going to be a problem with the voice because he wasn't singing too well. He was ill. It wasn't working out so we proceeded to Plan B, which was just to do the backing tracks and we did sixteen tracks there."

They decided to give Dave Gahan another chance to make it work. Martin and Fletch agreed to go New York's famous Electric Lady Studio in April to record the vocals. They thought that recording in Dave's new stomping ground of New York, and in one of rock 'n' roll's iconic studios, might help him.

"The Electric Lady sessions was like a six week adventure just to get Dave to do the vocals and make him feel at home," says Dave Clayton. "Go to New York, come on, let's give it some! It wasn't a particularly great studio, it's got a great legacy and memories, but it wasn't that amazing."

But even that didn't work. After four weeks of frustratingly little progress, Dave had only really recorded one usable vocal, 'Sister Of The Night'. Even that, he said later, he'd done while on heroin and it had to be pieced together from numerous takes. It was a far cry from the tremendous vocal performances he'd given when they were recording *Songs Of Faith And Devotion*. Ultimately Martin had to tell him to go home. They would carry on without him and hope he was able to finish his vocals later in the year. "We told him he had lost everything else in his life and now he was going to lose Depeche Mode as well," said Fletch.

Even more gallingly, they suggested that he get himself a vocal coach. They were sympathetic but there was also tremendous anger about what he was doing to the band, as well as what he was doing to himself. "Every time the phone went and someone said, 'It's about Dave', my first thought was always, *This is it, he's dead*," said Martin. "Which is not very nice."

It was impossible to argue with them. Dave knew he hadn't been delivering the kind of performances that he had in the past. He duly went back to LA and got in touch with vocal coach Evelyn Halus. His voice was technically OK but there was currently little depth to it. "It wasn't so much that I didn't have the ability to sing or anything," he said in a radio interview later, "it was like I couldn't find it inside my soul, I couldn't feel it in my heart. I was just doing my job, and it didn't feel good."

Martin and Fletch's tough love didn't work. Back in LA, Dave went on a massive drugs binge. In the early hours of May 28, at the Sunset Marquis hotel in LA he called a dealer and got him to prepare the cocktail of cocaine and heroin known as a 'speedball'. The heroin, he'd been told, was called Red Rum. He thought it was named after the famous Derby-winning horse. He didn't notice that it was actually 'murder' spelled backwards. He said later that he had a bad feeling even before he took the drug, asking the dealer not to fill the syringe right up. Nevertheless he injected it as he had so many times before and immediately started to black-out. "I saw myself lying on the floor with people running round me," he said later. "Then I remember total blackness and a lot of fear."

By the time the ambulance arrived, Dave was having a full-blown heart-attack. His heart ultimately stopped beating for two minutes in the back of the ambulance while they desperately tried to resuscitate him with jabs of adrenaline directly into the chest.

When he woke up, it was to find himself on a trolley in the hospital, handcuffed to a member of the LAPD. "Did I have another overdose," he groggily asked. "No, Dave," they replied. "You died."

"Not only did I die, I went to jail as well," he commented in a TV interview later. "That was not fun in Los Angeles, believe me. What I realised then was that I wanted to live."

Thankfully Martin and Fletch didn't get the telephone call they were dreading. In fact they didn't get a call at all. The news was released so quickly that they heard about this latest fall from grace on the radio like everybody else. Dave was still alive but, they wondered, for how much longer? They knew that addicts often have to hit the bottom before they can climb back up but it seemed like he'd hit the bottom many times before. There was no telling whether he'd be able to turn it around this time.

Manager Jonathan Kessler, by now one of Dave's best friends and someone he could totally rely on, came to bail him out. Outside there was a media scrum as he tried to give an impromptu press conference while Jonathan tried to drag him away into the waiting car. Unsurprisingly Dave looked half-dead with a scratched face and haunted eyes. As well as telling the assembled throng that he didn't want to be like Kurt Cobain he made a point of apologising to his mum. "My cat's lives are out," he admitted, "it's not a cool thing to be a drug addict."

When Martin and Fletch heard about it, not surprisingly they thought that the band was effectively over. They were right that Dave still hadn't learnt his lesson. He went back to the Sunset Marquis and it wasn't long before he was shooting up again. It seemed like for him that mythical concept, the bottom, just didn't exist. He was cushioned by his own wealth and fame.

"I was a very clever junkie," he said in the *Ultra* EPK in 1997. "I was able, for a very long period of time, to hide how bad I was. It's hard for you to hit the bottom. A financial bottom is something a lot of junkies hit when they have absolutely nothing left. When you're just sleeping on a mattress you've got to turn to someone for help, you've got to do something about it. The problem I had was an endless supply of money."

The band was the last thing on his mind. When Martin phoned him to suggest that they call it a day with Depeche Mode, it barely even registered. All of the other problems in his life had been forgotten about, rolled up into the single gigantic problem of drug addiction. In the end he said that it was trusted friend Jonathan Kessler's reaction that had the greatest impact on him. He'd always bailed him out and looked after him but this time he admitted that he didn't know what else they could do.

"If it wasn't for our manager, Jonathan Kessler, I probably wouldn't have made it," Dave said. "He saw me messed up yet again and said, 'I can't deal with this any more, I can't do this, and I'm not going to watch you doing this to yourself.'"

Jonathan called him to what he said was a meeting. When Dave got there he found that it was what therapists call an "intervention". Jonathan had hired a specialist called Bob Timmon who'd worked with many Hollywood addicts. They insisted that he had no choice but to go into a clinic – the Exodus Recovery Clinic in Marina Del Rey. His initial reaction was a stark "no way." Then he pleaded to be given more time, hoping for the opportunity to score. Finally he agreed to go later that afternoon. "So I went home, did my last deal, had my last little party and checked into the rehab," he told *Bong*.

Imposed rehab can sometimes be an unsuccessful method of dealing with addiction. Very few addicts give up because they're told to. Ominously, in addition to the world-leading company's many success stories, one of The Exodus Recovery clinic's former clients was Kurt Cobain and another was Blind Melon vocalist Shannon Hoon, who also checked out early and then died of an overdose.

Nevertheless Dave at last understood that he had to do things the hard way. Daniel Miller once said that one of Dave's major incentives was the American legal system. He was told that if he didn't go into rehab and then have tests for two years, he wouldn't be allowed in America anymore.

The first five days of treatment were simply gruelling cold turkey. He was tied to the bed and suffered terrible seizures. Then he went to the same kind of meetings that he'd attended before but this time he was at last ready to admit what heroin had done to him. More importantly he was listening to what the other addicts were saying and what he was being told by the counsellors. It had taken a long time but he realised that he'd hit rock bottom and he couldn't go any lower and survive. The Exodus was finally getting through to him – Dave Gahan was on his way back.

When he finally left the centre, the terms of his bail meant that he had to live in a "clean house" of ex-addicts in LA. It was an appropriately sobering experience to meet people who'd been through similar melt-downs without the cushion of wealth or, in some cases, friends or family.

It was brought home to him again how lucky he'd been when he heard of the death of the Smashing Pumpkins touring keyboardist Jonathan Melvoin, from a heroin overdose on July 12. From the treatment centre he tried to reiterate to *Melody Maker* how dangerous drugs could be.

"You don't have to be a life-time user," he said. "It only takes one time. People seem to believe the myth that if you just do it once you're fine, and now many people seem to be going straight to heroin, bypassing pot and all that and going straight to the devil. It's really scary."

At that point, although he had got his life back on track in terms of stopping the drugs, he seemed to have lost everything else. Teresa was pursuing a divorce. To top it off, he was required to present himself for two urine tests a week for the next two years. Nonetheless, he started to feel that he was on the way back up and if he could just stay clean this time everything would be alright.

# 17

# REHABILITATION

While Dave Gahan was slowly dragging himself out of the gutter, Martin was working on the new Depeche Mode album with Tim and the rest of Bomb The Bass, not knowing whether the vocals would ever be completed. "When we started this album, 90 per cent of the time I was still strung out, and the rest of the time I was sick from kicking," Dave said to the *Winnipeg Free Press*. "It became very obvious that physically I wasn't able to stand up in front of a microphone for more than an hour without wanting to lay down and die."

Fortunately, when he got out of the treatment centre, the vocal sessions with Evelyn Halus started to make a real difference. He had to admit that it was time to go back to basics. "I at first resented the hell out of it, because the idea was put to me and I was like, 'Hey wait a minute! I can sing! I don't need to be taught anything, I know it all,'" he said in a radio interview. "But you know what, it's just not true, because you never stop learning, in life, you never stop learning."

With his confidence slowly returning and his health coming back, he rejoined the rest of the band in London. They were working at the famous Abbey Road studios and they alternated between there and another studio, RAK, where Dave recorded his vocals over the course of a month. The change in him was both visible and audible. "I was dumbfounded when I saw him for the first time after he'd been in the clinic for a while," says Dave Clayton. "He looked *fantastic*. Nothing short of remarkable."

The atmosphere was much more relaxed now. He was clean and the band were more thoughtful to each other than they had been. The experiences of the last few months had caused some resentment but they also made them realise how important Depeche Mode was to them all.

"The three of us are pretty comfortable with each other once again," Dave said to *BAM* magazine afterwards. "I think the tension on the last record left such a deep scar that we weren't sure if we could get along anymore. The bottom line is that Martin and I both know that there's something we do together that works. We tried to put our differences aside and go in and do something positive."

Appropriately most of the songs on the record were dark, sombre affairs. The stand-out track was 'It's No Good'. They all knew that, with its powerful refrain and ultra-modern beats, it was potentially a huge hit. When Martin wrote it, he rang Fletch up excitedly and said, "I think I've written a Number 1."

"It was like, 'Oh yeah, that sounds like Depeche Mode!'" says Dave, "but I think the success in *Ultra* was that fact that we recorded the album – at all! And we managed to complete an album that we're all very happy with. And getting a hit on top of that always is, like, very nice."

There was tremendous relief that they'd made it and this alone meant the atmosphere was better than on *Songs Of Faith And Devotion*. "It's like almost a rebirth again," said Andy, "it's like it was fifteen years ago. It's that relaxed, you know?" "Abbey Road was like we were coming in to land," says Dave Clayton. "The optimism grew and grew and grew. Press came and we played them some tracks. You could see the international machine kicking in."

By this point Martin was describing their previous record as "a weird blip" in their series of electronic albums. He was clearly much more comfortable back in the familiar world of synthesisers and computerised sounds. But although Dave didn't feel able to criticise at that point, he wasn't quite so convinced. He felt, perhaps rightly, that their music had lost part of its character with the departure of Alan Wilder. For all the brilliance of Tim Simenon's production, it perhaps didn't quite have the Depeche Mode stamp to it.

"I felt a big part of what we were doing was missing – a leader, musically, and for me Alan was that," he said. "The others would say he was too controlling, but he just worked his arse off because he really believed in it and the idea of pushing himself musically, which you can hear on his own records. I find that really inspiring. I miss him."

When Alan left, Dave had been in his own world. He hadn't even responded to his calls. Now he wondered whether they could have persuaded him to stay if they'd tried harder. "I didn't respond to his leaving as much as I now realise I wanted to," he said to Q in 2003. "I really miss Alan's input on everything we do musically, but I miss him as a friend. He was probably the person in the band I felt supported by the most and I wish I'd fought harder for him to stay."

Amusingly one possible solution to the disappearance of Alan emerged at this time – the return of Vince. "Vince jokingly said that he would love to come back and replace Alan," Martin said to *Pavement*. "It was quite funny the first time he did it but by the fiftieth time we weren't quite sure whether he was joking or not. He literally said it to me so many times that I was thinking, *I think he's deadly serious*. But our music is so different these days, I couldn't see him fitting into what Depeche Mode do."

Inevitably the music on *Ultra* was over-shadowed on the album's release by the news of Dave's problems. During the interviews he gave at the time he was still in a state of shock at what he'd been through. He was determined to be completely honest and yet later he worried that he'd made it seem that he was the first person to go through drug addiction and overdose. It was certainly not his intention – quite the opposite in fact – but the lurid details, allied with his natural skill as a storyteller and raconteur, had journalists and readers of the music press hooked.

The band were uncomfortably aware that they'd got far more press from his overdose than they ever had from releasing records. "We got a double page in the *Sunday Times* magazine!" Fletch told *NME*. "Now, if we tried to get into the *Sunday Times* magazine for our music there'd be no way on this earth."

It was, maybe, a bit unfair on *Ultra*, which for all its faults had some great songs on it. Later on it would be described by Daniel Miller as a "transitional record". It was their first album without Alan Wilder since *A Broken Frame* and they weren't sure, yet, of the direction they were heading in. But, despite this, the trip-hop textures that Tim Simenon brought to it worked well with Martin's lyrics. They had none of the bravado or cheek of previous tracks like 'Master And Servant' or 'Behind The Wheel'. Instead they were resigned and world-weary. As always he seemed to be in sync with Dave's emotional state, whether he consciously wrote like that or not. Part of it, of course, was that their problems were more challenging than either of them at times admitted.

"I would hate to see him lose everything like I did before I realised," Dave told *NME*'s Keith Cameron. "So I think Martin is writing these songs and he can't help but think about what's been going on with me and then maybe look at himself in the mirror. That's the way it works."

Dave also found it difficult at times to cope with the fact that Martin and Fletch could still have a drink while he couldn't. "I feel like the odd one out," he said. For him drink and even drugs had always started out as a social thing. It was only in the end with heroin that it had become a solitary vice.

"From the start of Depeche Mode, Fletch and Martin were obviously real friends," Dave told *The Times* in 2001. "They went to school together and I was the odd one out, and basically I've continued to be the odd one out throughout the whole life of Depeche Mode. We're very different personalities and I know Fletch and Martin hang out, but I don't think we'd ever hang out as a band. We do occasionally go to the pub and have a drink together, but that's it really. But that's alright, I'm OK with that now."

But in the past alcohol and drugs had sometimes been a way for Dave to bond with the band. Dave treasured one memory he had of Martin's appreciation of their relationship. It was after a gig in Chile, they'd recently heard about the death of Kurt Cobain and they were in what Dave described as their "I love you" mode.

"You know, Mart said something really wonderful to me one night, when we were a little bit intoxicated, let's say, on the last tour," he said. "But it stuck in my mind, and whether he meant it or not, it was a beautiful thing to say. He said that he got his songs from God, but that he had to channel them through me. And that was the message that he got. And it made me feel really great, and so I just keep hold of that, that's how it works."

They were very different characters and yet the ride they'd been on for the last few years was in itself a bond between them. Nobody else except the four members knew what it was like to be in Depeche Mode, and the complex relationship between the two of them was always at the heart of the band. Over the years it had become impossible to tell when Martin's writing was inspired by Dave, and when he was merely feeling exactly the same emotions.

"Depeche Mode is Martin's songs and my voice," he said. "The music is very much head music and then I bring the heartbeat."

The first half of *Ultra* was a kind of cross between *Violator* and *Songs Of Faith And Devotion*. It has the slick production of the former but in 'Barrel Of A Gun' and 'It's No Good', particularly, there's the aggressive edge of the latter. Dave's voice, though, is very different. It's much dreamier and more resigned. He's not laidback and confident like he was on *Violator* or impassioned and driven like he was on *Songs Of Faith And Devotion*. It's the sound of a man who's only just come up for air.

On the second half of the album, things stretch out and become even less direct. They've still got the bluesiness of the previous two albums but it's closer to the blues of Tricky or Massive Attack. There are few pop hooks. On the *101* video Martin was seen going into a shop in Nashville and buying up arm-loads of country music. The result seems to come out in 'The Bottom Line'. They brought celebrated session musician BJ Cole in to play slide guitar on it and, if not exactly country, it's the closest they'd got.

"I was talking to Martin during the session and he was raving about the steel guitar work on [legendary Nashville songwriter] Ray Price records," says BJ now, "and that was what inspired them to ask me to come in and work on it. It was a record called 'Night Life', which I remember him enthusing about. That's one of my favourite records as well."

Although it might not have been country, *Ultra* was certainly an album that's metaphorically sitting on a porch contemplating mortality. They still hadn't quite worked out what had happened to them over the last few years but they'd managed to get another great album out. For now, that was enough. The album's title came out of a feeling almost of defiance. Its slick, positive feel hardly fits the music on the record or the way their lives had been going over the last few years but they were all determined to put a brave face on things. "The title really fits in with our new line-up," Martin said. "We lost a member along the way and now it's the new, improved, slimmed-down version. I think it's a great, positive title."

Some reviewers were disappointed that *Ultra* appeared to be business as usual, expecting some kind of musical version of Dave's interviews, perhaps. "Issues are skirted, poetry is attempted and we're left clutching another instalment of stadium-orientated angst, at a time when we were expecting reflective intimacy," said *NME*.

After the coincidence of *Violator* appearing just as electronic music got big, it did seem like they'd gone back to their usual path of appearing a little out-of-time. In 1997 The Prodigy went to Number 1 in the States with *The Fat Of The Land*. There was much talk about a new electronic invasion, which never quite materialised. Depeche Mode should have seemed like forefathers of that scene but *Ultra* was slower and more thoughtful. Despite this, if not all the critics were convinced, many fans welcomed the return to their roots after the rockisms of *Songs Of Faith And Devotion*. *Ultra* didn't sell as well as their previous two records but, considering they didn't tour to promote it, it didn't do bad at all.

They were, at least, starting to have fun again and this came across in the first singles to be released from the album. 'Barrel Of A Gun' was a blast of raw defiance. It was much more straightforward than most of what they'd done in the last few years. It also saw Martin tentatively admitting, for the first time, that he was writing from Dave's perspective. It was hard to avoid that with its powerful metaphor of facing up to death. But he also pointed out that it was about his own life and the problems he'd been through himself.

In the video Anton focused directly on the figure of 'lost' Dave who'd emerged so graphically in the interviews he gave at that time. It begins with what seems to be cold turkey imagery, with the singer writhing around on his bed unable to get any peace. Then, with eyes painted on his eyelids to give the impression that he's awake, he stumbles through the streets, before appearing to stare blankly at the ceiling as Fletch and Martin fall asleep on his shoulder. It was one of Anton's darkest videos but also, as usual, with a vein of pitch black humour.

For the 'It's No Good' video, though, Anton went the other way and mocked his rock star persona. "I think that was probably one of the most fun videos that I've ever made," Dave said afterwards. He was dressed up as a faded rocker, with a 1950s quiff and gold lamè, a has-been who doesn't realise that times have moved on. With his cheesy winks to the crowd and exaggerated rock star posing, it was a chance for him to prove that he'd got back one of the things that heroin had taken away: his sense of humour. But then it was easy for him to laugh because *Ultra* had proved that they were almost as big as ever, even when operating, as they saw it, on half-power. It would have been even bigger but this time they all agreed that it would be crazy to go on tour again. For the first time they put their health and well-being above being on the road.

"It's not just David, it's all of us," Fletch said to *The Sunday Times*. "Dave is still at a tender time of his recovery. And we don't want to put too much pressure on him. Touring puts a lot of pressure on him, it takes a lot of time. We just want to enjoy this year, promote the album, have a successful album and say we enjoyed ourselves."

After 'It's No Good' they released two more singles, 'Home' and 'Useless'. The latter was significant for being the last video they'd shoot with Anton Corbijn for eight years. It wasn't the best they'd ever made together, mostly focusing on Dave singing in a gravel pit as Martin and Fletch lounge on a car behind him. The twist at the end, when it's revealed they're directly singing to somebody, doesn't quite make up for the slightly dull visuals all the way through. However, there wasn't any suggestion at all that they were disappointed with what he'd done for them. It was just that changing things every now and then was part of their longevity. 'Useless' is notable for the fact that Dave is starting to look slightly healthier, after his post-drug abuse appearances in 'Barrel of A Gun' and 'It's No Good'. There was, however, still a long way to go.

# 18

# CLEAN

After he started to recover, Dave began running religiously. He decided to stay in New York where his new girlfriend Jennifer lived and slowly his old self came back. He'd begun to see Los Angeles as a kind of monster and it was a relief to be somewhere without the trappings of ostentatious rock 'n' roll.

"Los Angeles can eat you alive," he said to *Detour* in 1997. "It's an easier place to withdraw, and once you get into that place it's very difficult to get out and be around people. Here, I can look out of my window and see life going on 24-hours a day."

More importantly in New York he had more of a life himself. He had an apartment near Central Park and a new kind of freedom. Having lived the 'rock star' life for a while, suddenly the domesticity that had been so chafing back in Essex was very welcome. Jennifer had a son and as their relationship deepened he was able to experience a new version of the family life that he'd left behind back in England. He felt that she loved him for himself, rather than for the rock star that he'd become. "I could see something in her I wanted," he said. "She didn't give a crap about the band I was in. She just genuinely cared about what I was doing to myself and I saw that right from the start."

Normality was a joy in itself and, clean for about a year, he was starting to feel self-conscious about the revelatory interviews he'd given about his drug abuse. He worried that what was supposed to be a warning could be seen as just another sensationalised story of the so-called 'rock 'n' roll' lifestyle. He was also conscious that his son Jack was now reaching an age where he'd be able to read the magazine articles for himself.

"I find now that it's too taxing on the people that care a lot about me like my family, my son," he said on America's *The Tonight Show*. "He's old enough to pick up the papers and read. Sometimes stuff is really kind of glamorised or it gets kind of portrayed sort of in the wrong kind of light and that's why I was trying to kind of very graphically explain that it's not cool and it's not fun and it's a complete kind of clichéd way to live, especially being in a rock band. But you can change it, you can turn it around."

Despite this, the tussle between his domestic side and the performer wasn't over yet. It was just a question of finding a balance. When they played a few TV shows to promote *Ultra*, he found himself missing the huge live performances they'd had throughout the 1990s. He also felt a need for the kind of creative outlet that he'd never had before. It had always been enough for him to interpret Martin's songs but, having been through so much turmoil, he wanted to express himself. Also, this time it would be a long wait until the new batch of material from Martin. They all needed a break after what they'd been through in the 1990s. In 1998 they were in a mood to look back on what they'd achieved. Dave now felt well enough to go back on the road and so they released a second singles collection, *Singles 1986>98*.

As they had with the previous singles collection, they added a new track 'Only When I Lose Myself'. It was a slow, almost stately song with a kind of dignity that perhaps they felt they'd lost with all the press in the last few years. It almost harked back to their *Violator* sound. As a nod towards their history they got Brian Griffin to do the artwork and the video this time. He was pleasantly surprised to find that they were a very different band than the kids he'd worked with so many years before.

"I was most impressed by David Gahan when he came out of his drug phase," says Brian. "I found him very level-headed and very clever and a very nice man to be with. He was the focus of the band for me. He was a very commendable person. I liked him a lot. I can't remember him being as focused as Martin and Fletch during my early period of working with them in the early 1980s. I seem to remember them being more focused on the cover than David was. But when I met them again in 2000 for that promo he was the one who was focused."

The singles tour was very different to *World Violation* or *Devotional*. Backstage was a strictly drugs free zone and only beer or wine was allowed. They were a changed touring animal from the swirl of excess during the *Songs Of Faith And Devotion* days.

## DEPECHE MODE & THE SECOND COMING

They also wisely didn't go for the 100+ dates of previous tours but, nevertheless, it was still sixty sold-out shows. It was encouraging for them to play the old singles and hear for themselves how much progress they'd made musically over the last twelve years. These shows didn't have the grandiose sets of previous tours, either. They stripped things down and abandoned any pretensions to being 'rock stars'.

At times this must have been difficult. Particularly as some of their fans seemed to have such high expectations of them. This time they started the dates in the former Eastern Bloc and the reaction was startling. They played Estonia, then Latvia and then their first ever date in Russia after so long talking about it. It was a country where they'd had a devoted following for fifteen years and the long wait had sharpened fans' appetites. As in Hungary, many fans went to extreme lengths to look like their idols. More bizarrely for the band, perhaps, it wasn't how they looked now but how they'd looked many years before.

"When we were in Russia there was a fan that waited outside the hotel the entire time we were there," said Martin in a TV interview, "and he looked exactly like I did in the 1980s – with the same hairstyle and clothes. The funny thing was, she was a woman. We then began calling her Martina whenever we saw her."

That level of adulation wasn't necessarily what Dave needed. One of the things that his addiction counsellors had taught him was the need to remove himself from his old way of life and his old, drug-using friends. This had proved easy enough in that he'd moved from LA to New York and his former "drug buddies" had lost interest in him since he kicked the habit. However, touring with Depeche Mode again must have rekindled old memories of the *Devotional* tour. Although backstage was now 'clean', inevitably it wasn't the controlled environment that he could enjoy at home.

However, the tour did remind them all how much they loved playing live. It had been a long time since their last proper jaunt. Apart from a couple of low-key dates to promote *Ultra*, they'd not been back on the road since Dave leapt from the stage and went crashing into the barrier in Indianapolis almost four years before. "It was great," said Fletch, "a real buzz. We felt like a band again, no stupid arguments, no ego-ridden rubbish. We couldn't wait to get back into the studio."

They were given another boost by the release of the *For The Masses* tribute album. If they'd been surprised to find their music being cited as an inspiration by the pioneers of techno, this was just as unexpected. A whole host of rock bands such as Rammstein, Deftones and Monster Magnet delivered covers of Depeche Mode tracks. They'd picked up on almost exactly the opposite aspects of the band's music to Derrick May and the other producers. They were interested in the darkness, the heavy, industrial side. Rammstein's take on 'Stripped' became particularly celebrated among their fans and Marilyn Manson, who wasn't able to contribute to *For The Masses*, later recorded his own version of 'Personal Jesus'. Perhaps most inspiringly The Cure recorded a version of 'World In My Eyes'. When they started out one of Depeche Mode's main aims had been to make records as good as The Cure's. They shared similar roots in suburbia and, despite many differences, there was a certain shared aesthetic and certainly many shared fans.

In 1999 Dave married Jennifer and adopted her son Jimmy. He even converted to her religion, Greek-Orthodox, in order to marry in a Greek-Orthodox church. It was the start of one of the happiest periods in his life. He became a father again, to a baby daughter, Stella, and he was able to relax and enjoy the material success that Depeche Mode had brought, as well as the success of being clean. They lived in a nice, tenth floor apartment with views overlooking the River Hudson and at last he felt at home.

"I feel so proud of my son, Jack, and when I go home my stepson throws his arms around me and my little baby daughter gives me that look – that's what it's all about," he said to *Time Out*. "It sounds soppy but I really feel loved. I'm working on myself; I'm still very distrusting and stuff but I get these massive moments when it's just like absolute bliss."

Many of his new friends in New York had been through similar experiences with addiction, which helped. At the start of 2000 he also met Alan Wilder again for the first time since he'd left Depeche Mode. It was a happy reunion for both of them. After the initial shock of his departure, Dave had always been very complimentary about Alan in the press and the keyboard player, now working on his own revered project Recoil, appreciated it. While doing promo for Recoil's debut album *Liquid* in New York, he and Hepzibah went to visit Dave, Jennifer and their new baby.

In 1999, Martin was struggling to write the next album. For the first time he had something close to writer's block. By then Depeche Mode had sold something like 50 million records and they were all approaching the end of their thirties. Perhaps there wasn't the sense of urgency that there had been when they were younger. "I started working on songs about a year and a half ago, and I struggled," he said to *Billboard*. "I spent the first six months doing nothing. I couldn't get motivated. I couldn't come up with an idea that worked for me. It was actually quite frightening."

In the end, Martin asked for help. He called engineer Gareth Jones and keyboard player Paul Freeguard to come in to the studio and work with him. Having other people there to play his initial ideas proved less intimidating than he'd thought. It was a kind of pressure but at that point he needed it. With people hanging around waiting to hear what he'd come up with he didn't feel able to slacken off. After an alarming burglary at his Hertfordshire home, the songwriter then moved to Santa Barbara in Southern California with his wife. The three members of Depeche Mode were now thousands of miles apart. Nevertheless in their own ways they were all preparing for the next album. Dave was still regularly practising the vocal exercises that Evelyn Halus had given him and when Martin was finally finished, things were much smoother than they had been on the last two records.

When they met up to discuss their next record it was a revelation. They were able to sit in a room together and talk about what they wanted without someone having to be there to mediate. "Often our manager would have had to come to each one individually and talk to us about things," Martin said to *Virtually Alternative* at the time. "There was all kinds of weird stuff going on like that. Now we're able to sit down and talk, which is important – communication is always important between any group of people."

To emphasise their continuing move away from the rockist "blip" of *Songs Of Faith And Devotion*, they approached Mark Bell of techno act LFO to produce. He'd recently been acclaimed for his work on Bjork's *Homogenic* album and, like Tim Simenon, he'd been inspired by Depeche Mode's earlier work as a kid. Pretty soon songs started coming together and they prepared to start recording. It would be a significant milestone, their first post-heroin album. It was also a chance for Dave to remind the world that he was a great singer, not just another rock star drug casualty.

"Let's face it," he continued. "When you've reached the unfortunate point where you've nearly ended your life – and the world's been watching the entire time – there comes a minor need to establish and affirm, if only to yourself, that you can still get the job done."

Depeche Mode were a band with a powerful work ethic and this had been their longest gap in between studio albums. The songs Martin had written, as always, were oblique in their meaning but some specifically referenced the things they'd been through. In 'The Dead Of Night', for example, he has Dave sing of the "zombie room", his phrase for the VIP rooms in clubs where people take drugs and lose their personalities. "While you're there, all these people in the room are your best mates in the world," Martin said. "But the next day, if you bump into one of them on the street, you won't even know their name."

Mark Bell encouraged Dave to record the vocals in the studio on his own, to give them a more intimate feel. It suited the sound of the album, which, in places, was almost ambient. At times, as on 'Breathe', he sounded almost like a torch singer, some kind of chanteuse from the 1940s or 1950s. This had always been part of Martin's aesthetic. He described another track 'When The Body Speaks' as "the Righteous Brothers playing next door to a rave."

Even more than *Ultra,* this latest album – entitled *Exciter* – sounded tired, exhausted even, but not in a bad way. If the previous albums had been about partying, this was the chill-out room. At the time Dave said that he felt able to contribute more than he had in the past. He was putting forward his own ideas without feeling inhibited. The word they all used for the sessions later was "laid-back" and, in retrospect, the singer seemed to think that they'd gone too far in that direction. While working on the demos Martin sometimes had group meditation sessions with Gareth Jones and Paul Freeguard and they'd tried to make things as relaxed as possible.

# DEPECHE MODE & THE SECOND COMING

On 'When The Body Speaks' Dave tapped into this vibe singing, he said, as though he was holding his baby daughter in his arms.

There was much less of a band feel than there had been on *Violator* and *Songs Of Faith And Devotion*. Instead Martin collaborated with Mark Bell and his team while Dave was left to put forward his ideas and sing. "One of the main differences is that there is a lot less performance," Martin said, "but that's also probably dictated by the songs more." At the time, perhaps, a more laid-back vibe was exactly what they needed. There were still tracks like 'The Dead Of The Night', with its industrial grind that took things in more of an aggressive direction. And 'Dream On' was another great, slick pop single with some of Martin's best lyrics. Overall, though, the album is most conspicuous for its gentle, drifting feel. There was little of the stridency that they were known for. At times it was almost a cosy record. They'd grown used to each other, seen each other at their worst and accepted it. That comes across in the music.

"It's like a family thing, really," said Fletch to *Virtually Alternative*. "We don't spend every minute of our lives together because we've got our own families and friends. I figure we've grown to respect each other's idiosyncrasies as well. We know each other well in that way and that's a good thing."

Fletch also pointed out that it was a record where the word 'love' appeared in four different song titles. It wasn't a complete break from the type of relationships that Martin had described in 'Behind The Wheel' and 'Master And Servant' but there was certainly something a bit less extreme going on. Not everybody in the media liked that but, listened to as a whole, *Exciter* has a beautifully warm, dream-like feel. Its distance from where they were just five years before with *Songs Of Faith And Devotion* is best demonstrated by the last track, 'Goodnight Lovers'. It has a trace of the gospel influence that they first unveiled on that album and yet its much more gentle. It's not evangelical, it's more like a lullaby.

With the second single 'I Feel Loved', though, they made explicit reference to the aspect of their music that had gone missing. They covered legendary proto-punks The Stooges' track 'Dirt' on the b-side. This was the kind of music that had got Dave into being in a band in the first place and yet with *Exciter* they were a very long way from punk rock.

# DAVE GAHAN

The name *Exciter* may seem highly ironic, it's not Depeche Mode's most exciting record but neither was it a total failure. It just took people a while to get used to a version of Depeche Mode that sounded, almost, contented. "With each record we've recorded, I've felt that each one is more optimistic than the last one," Dave said. On tour, though, the arch showman must have been conscious that these new songs couldn't dominate stadiums and arenas like their old ones. As Alexis Petridis in *The Guardian* put it in a review of their Wembley Arena show: "Tonight, Depeche Mode are at their best when they abandon all subtlety and perform songs as overblown as Gahan's posturing. As the grinding sleaze of 'I Feel You' and 'Personal Jesus' lurch forth, both his outrageous hamming and Marilyn Manson's love of Depeche Mode make perfect sense."

# 19

# PAPER MONSTERS

Dave's slightly jaundiced view of *Exciter* may have been coloured by the fact that, in breaks between the sessions, he was already starting to work on his own songs. He felt inwardly somewhat unsatisfied. The way Depeche Mode worked, taking sounds and manipulating them with computer technology, meant it was inherently difficult for him to contribute to the recording process.

He very tentatively suggested that, maybe, one of the songs could go on a Depeche Mode album but it was handled in a typically awkward fashion. He waited until Martin had been drinking one night and then played him some of them. "Martin made some comments," Fletch told *Q,* "and when he'd sobered up he couldn't remember what he'd said." Dave didn't want to push things. In the rigid world of Depeche Mode, the idea of Martin no longer writing all the songs was a sizable earthquake. They'd been so successful by that point that to make such a dramatic change was hard to imagine. And Dave wasn't sure it was Depeche Mode songs he wanted to write anyway. He had a hankering to do something that was much more raw, a garage band where the music would be created in a more live environment. In 2001, bands like The Strokes were breaking through and simple, three chord rock 'n' roll was the most fashionable sound in the world again. This was the sort of music he'd liked as a teenager but it wasn't something that he'd ever seriously considered bringing to Depeche Mode. Nor had he thought about a solo record for most of the time he'd been in the band. He even mocked solo-album syndrome in a Danish TV interview in 1990: "One of the main reasons why bands split up is because big egos build up," he says, "and someone thinks they're much better than the rest of them and goes off and makes their own record. They usually come crawling back and [say] 'Let's make a record again.'"

Of course it wasn't the case that he thought he was "much better" than Martin when he came to record his own solo album. It was more that the whole purpose of making music – to express yourself – was starting to become less rewarding for him in Depeche Mode. In the past he'd been satisfied with the adulation of the crowd when they played live but, since the *Devotional* tour, he'd started to need something else.

When he was living in LA he often told people that he wanted to do something different to Depeche Mode but he was of course in no state to bring his ideas to fruition. By the time they recorded *Ultra*, he was still trying to find space for himself within the band. He'd written one tune called 'The Ocean Song' but Martin diplomatically said that although he liked it, the song didn't fit with the other tracks on the album. After the 'Singles 86-98' tour finished, Dave had again talked about making a solo album but then there was the making of *Exciter* to consider.

Dave and a drummer friend of his, Victor Endrizzio, had often talked about working together. Victor suggested that he should also talk to a friend of his, Knox Chandler. Dave knew of Knox, who also lived in New York and he'd brought him in to do the string arrangements and play the cello on 'When The Body Speaks' on *Exciter*. Knox was a very successful session musician, he'd worked with Psychedelic Furs and Siouxsie And The Banshees among others. When they first met, though, it was purely by chance.

"I happened to walk into a place and he was there," Dave told a webzine. "So something possessed me at that point. It was really nerve-racking, but I went up to him and just said, 'I'm Dave Gahan, I hear you play guitar and some cello and stuff and I've got these song ideas and I need someone to help me develop them.' And he was all just like, 'Yeah, great'. He said, 'I've got a little work room in my house, come over next week.'"

As they started working together, Dave's concept of how his music should sound started to change. He was listening to all kinds of new records, including the blues albums that Daniel Miller gave him. "[Daniel] said to me, 'Look, if you like this, then you've got to listen to this!'" Dave said to *VH1*. "So I got introduced to John Lee Hooker, Muddy Waters and Howlin' Wolf. Muddy Waters blew my head off! He still does. I can play my guitar to it. It's all twelve bar stuff and you can have a lot of fun. I play my harmonica over Howlin' Wolf's stuff. It's like going backwards for me. It's great to go back, because you suddenly realise, 'Oh, Willie Dixon wrote that Zeppelin song!'"

Another experience that could have been either revelatory or intimidating for him was when Johnny Cash covered 'Personal Jesus' for his *American IV: The Man Comes Around* album. Johnny Cash had a habit of taking songs and making the definitive versions of them. Trent Reznor of Nine Inch Nails had already experienced that when Cash's version of his 'Hurt' became more celebrated in many quarters than the original. Dave, though, was simply awestruck. He was a huge fan of Johnny Cash and felt that the cover was an honour for the band and for Martin in particular. "Martin was all like, 'Yeah, I guess it's pretty good,'" he said to *Rolling Stone* "and I said, 'Martin, this is like Elvis covering one of your songs!'"

It was some competition for Dave's version but perhaps it helped that they were so different. Nevertheless it was an intriguing glimpse of a different way of working. The kind of soulful, gravelly quality that Johnny Cash possessed was something that Dave had been aspiring towards for years.

Dave would go round to Knox's apartment and sing him the words and melodies that he came up with. Later on, when he didn't have vocals to do during the *Exciter* sessions, he would work on his own songs, sending them to Knox who would add his own elements and send them back.

Often Knox's suggestion of how the songs should sound was much more spacious and dynamic than Dave had expected. One song, for example, 'Black And Blue Again', ended up having an almost epic feel with Knox's cello. It was a very direct apology to his wife Jennifer for an argument they'd had. He wrote the words in the back of a cab as he was driven across New York. "We had a huge fight, and I walked out of our apartment," he said. "I was on my way to the studio when it suddenly dawned on me that I was the one in the wrong. That song is basically me admitting that I'm not always a very nice person. I realised that relationships weren't easy, and I had to change."

Having been through the experience of addiction therapy, which was partly about recognising when he was lying to himself, honesty was hugely important. "There were times when I felt like a fraud in Depeche Mode," he said. "Even though I identified with Martin's songs, I was always interpreting someone else's feelings." This came across in another song, 'Dirty Sticky Floors', which addressed his darkest moments with black humour. "'Dirty Sticky Floors' is the whole lifestyle that I was drawn into," he said in an interview for website *Home Taping Is Killing Music*. "That whole kind of rock star cliché … was a lot of fun for some time and then it wasn't any more, so out of the ashes of that came 'Dirty Sticky Floors' which really was a piss-take of myself and the sort of whole glamorous side of – it's not really glamorous at all – but that whole culture of the rock and roll star that gets drunk, gets high, and falls on his face and usually ends up on some dirty sticky floor."

This track was also the song that mentioned the Tin Man and the Cowardly Lion, the sole amusing story to come out of Dave's long nightmare in LA. "I wanted to get rid of the negativity that has surrounded me," he said. "One thing that kept me going was my sense of humour – and I wanted to reflect that." He wasn't just inspired by the events of six years before. One song, the beautiful, gentle 'Stay' was about the birth of his daughter. Another, 'Hidden Houses', was inspired by walking around the old meat-packing district near his home with his stepson Jimmy, looking at all the little alleys and wondering where they led to. Another song 'A Little Piece' he literally wrote while walking down the street, singing into a Dictaphone. As people looked at him in confusion, he sang virtually the whole song and then went home and played the tape to Knox over the phone.

He found the excitement of the city much easier to cope with than the slow pace of LA. In LA there wasn't enough background noise. He said that all he could hear was the "committee in my head". One of the few ways he'd found to soothe it was through the music of Sigur Ros. He'd become obsessed with the Icelandic band's second album *Ágætis byrjun*, which he said he'd been carrying around "like a Bible" while writing the songs. When it was time to go into the studio then, he decided to approach their English producer Ken Thomas. Ken had done a remix of Depeche Mode's 'A Question Of Time' and he was well known for his sublime engineering skills. Daniel Miller knew him and sent him some of the early demos and they arranged to meet up for a meal in New York.

## DEPECHE MODE & THE SECOND COMING

Initially Dave was nervous. He wasn't sure how a respected producer like Ken Thomas would take the idea of him aspiring to be a songwriter after all these years. He decided to lay his cards on the table. "He said to me, 'I'm not a lyricist, I left school at 15, I'm not Bob Dylan. This is what you get,'" Ken remembers now. "I asked Ken what he thought and he said to me, 'Your songs really make me feel good, I'd really like to do it,'" Dave said. "And that to me, that's what I want to do, I want to make a record that makes people feel good."

Initially they went with Knox and drummer Victor Indrizzo into the Empire View studios in New York to start pre-production. The lyrics did, indeed, need some work. They were dealing with very rough demos that he and Knox had written at his kitchen table. "Some of the lyrics changed," Ken says. "They were just too obvious at the beginning. It changed a lot because a lot of it was too cheesy. It just wasn't focused enough. They needed working."

When they first played the early demos to Daniel Miller, the Mute boss wasn't convinced. He thought that Dave needed to write more songs. Ken recalls: "When I spoke to Dan Miller afterwards he said to me, 'Ken, I don't want an LA album. I want an album that you can do, a more English album'. Initially I thought Dave wanted to do an Iggy Pop album but I think that was not going to be released on Mute records. I don't think Mute wanted anything like that. Daniel couldn't put out an album that didn't fit into his Mute catalogue. And it's a big machine, Depeche Mode, so there was probably a lot of political things going on."

When they went into a bigger New York studio, Electric Lady, they began reshaping the songs, trying to retain their raw, intimate quality while giving them a new dynamism. Dave was in an unusual position during the making of his first solo album. It was the eleventh album he'd worked on and yet in some ways he was an absolute beginner. This was the first time he'd ever been immersed in the making of a record to this extent. "Dave was involved in working on the songs all the way through," says Ken. "He'd arrive every morning and leave when we'd finished at night. Which he'd never ever done on a whole album." As a songwriter he had been schooled by the hundreds of live shows that he'd played with Depeche Mode. It had taught him what works and what doesn't. He knew all about crafting big, sing-a-long choruses.

"His strength is that he's used to singing to lots of people so he knows how to get a song to engage," says Ken. "All the vocals were done quite quickly. He'd been doing it for so long. But he wasn't coming over as a big songwriter. It was just stories that he was telling really."

Dave enjoyed the experience far more than he had working on *Exciter*. Apart from anything else there wasn't the pressure that was always present on a Depeche Mode album. "It's quite exciting when you make a record like that," said Ken. "You don't have to worry about if it's going to sell any records, Dave didn't, he just wanted to make an album that he could put on and be chuffed with, really. All he wanted was to have the record released and be able to go on tour. We weren't really worried about anything except making an album that he could switch on and be really proud of. He was happy all the time because he was doing what he wanted to do. I think if you find someone who's doing what they want to do then they are happy. It was just a very nice feeling the whole way through the recording."

It was also very clear to Ken that the singer's sense of humour had fully returned. He spent much of his time in the studio telling stories about the black days of his addiction and about his recovery. "He'd come back with stories about the rehab meetings that he used to go to twice a week but it was always very jokey," says the producer. "He had so many stories about Depeche Mode but unfortunately I can't tell you any of them! They're a big band and big bands always end up with that kind of Metallica vibe, like a dysfunctional family. I think there's always a comedy element to Dave Gahan with everything he does. I think even when he performs, he says he doesn't take it too seriously. There was a lot of taking the mickey out of me or Knox."

Another song, 'Bottle Living', was a furious assault on alcoholism. It was addressed to somebody who, he felt, needed to get help to deal with alcohol. It could have been a reference to himself and his own past habits. Lost in all the publicity for his struggle with heroin was the fact that he had an almost as regular penchant for alcohol in the mid-1990s. "It's a struggle with that stuff, especially the drinking," he said in a Swedish TV interview in 2002. "We have these crutches in life but I can honestly say I haven't had a drink in seven years."

The album hadn't turned out how he thought it would when he was looking for an outlet for his 'rock' instincts. It had, however, achieved its main objective, which was to be an album driven by people rather than by technology. He wanted to play in a band in a much more traditional sense. It was more than five years since his overdose and he was starting to remember the good things about his life on the West Coast, the bands he'd seen and the excitement of American rock 'n' roll.

"There'd always been a strong contingent within Depeche who were very against going down the 'rock' road," he said to Chris Roberts in *Uncut*. "Everything I fancied was always 'too rock', y'know? I was bored with that. To me, it was like: 'Well, that's another door you've closed, guys.' They thought I wanted to turn them into Guns N' Roses or something ... and yes, there was definitely a part of me that did!"

Despite the evident feelings of tension within Depeche Mode, he generously gave the band's songwriter credit for the way his own songs turned out. "I've had a lot of training from somebody who I respect who is probably one of the best songwriters of my time, who is of course Martin," he said, "and that's definitely rubbed off on me."

Ken Thomas sees Dave's solo debut album – entitled *Paper Monsters* – as essentially another step in his recovery programme. It was about learning to deal with his own problems and making the best of his life. From listening to a band like Sigur Ros, who'd come to mean so much to him, he wanted to make a record that would express his own feelings, whatever they might be.

"I think he used Sigur Ros as therapy and he was trying to make an album that was therapeutic to him as well, that he could listen to and feel slightly spiritual," says Ken. "It was a big thing for him to do his own album. He was starting at the beginning. He had no big budget, he had no big studio, there was no budget for expensive session musicians or anything like that. He was starting again. It wasn't like a superstar having a big budget to do his own album. It wasn't like that at all."

Despite his vast experience as part of Depeche Mode, *Paper*

# DAVE GAHAN

*Monsters* was, in some ways, a typical debut album. It was the expression of years of pent-up emotions. All the things he hadn't been able to say during his time in the band came out. There was no one underlying theme or even sound. It was sonically all over the map and yet, with the help of Knox and Ken Thomas, there were some genuinely moving songs there.

Part of the excitement of recording *Paper Monsters* was not knowing how it would turn out. With Depeche Mode he felt like everything was so carefully planned that there was little room for spontaneity anymore. *Violator* had turned out very differently than he expected but, since then, he felt they'd fallen into a way of working where most of the creative work was done in front of a computer screen. It wasn't easy for him to have the kind of control that he wanted in that environment.

After so much success with Depeche Mode there was widespread scepticism that the frontman could suddenly turn his hand to songwriting. However, the media underestimated his determination. He'd been writing songs for far longer than anybody thought. It was just that in the past he hadn't had the confidence to show them to anybody.

Now, though, he felt like he'd at last had a chance to grow up a bit. Just for a moment he toyed with calling the album *Essex Boy*, in a humorous nod to how far he'd come. As Alan and Daniel used to say on occasion, you could take the boys out of Basildon but you couldn't take Basildon out of the boys. In the end, though, he went for *Paper Monsters* – a reference to the insecurities that had driven him for many years.

"Even when I was a kid I spent a lot of time wondering who was in the closet and who was under the bed, footsteps chasing me in the night," he said in an interview for *Paper Monsters* press promos, "and all those kind of dreams I used to have as a kid and to be honest, I realised a lot of what stops me from what I want to do is just fear. I think that stops a lot of people doing what they want to do, or saying what they want to say. I think that's one of the hardest things in the world to admit to yourself."

The recording of the album caused schisms in the Depeche Mode fan community worldwide. They were deeply loyal to the group and many of them were disappointed with what they perceived as a lack of loyalty to each other. There had been widespread dismay when Alan Wilder left and now it seemed like the band might be falling apart.

"It's unbelievable," said Dave to *Metro* of the fans' reaction. "The obsession sometimes gets a bit crazy. It's definitely divided a lot of fans. A lot of the hardcore have turned their back on me, and I knew that would happen, but there's nothing I can do about that. I have to do what I feel's right in my heart." On the other hand he did have some support. He was encouraged to receive a beautifully laid out book from an American fan with dozens of emails of encouragement in it. "At least I have a hundred fans there that are definitely gonna buy the record," he said, "so I've got a start."

Most of the reviews for the album were relatively noncommittal. Few critics raved about it and yet it wasn't dismissed. *Q* described it as "superior to both the last two Mode albums and [Martin] Gore's recent solo effort, *Counterfeit 2*."

The consensus was that it was good, but that Depeche Mode were better. "Gahan's vocal can still elevate the dumbest lyric to the level of a cathartic mantra," remarked *Pitchfork*, "a skill that comes handy in the absence of Martin Gore."

When *Paper Monsters* was released, it was encouragingly successful. Inevitably it didn't shift as many units as a Depeche Mode album but it proved there was a large audience for him. In June 2003 he let out a little more steam with a solo tour. This, again, proved his personal popularity. He played enormous venues in Eastern Europe and two nights at the Shepherd's Bush Empire in London. As a further indication of his 'rock' credentials he also played Glastonbury Festival, something Depeche Mode had never done. This included a version of 'Personal Jesus' which was a hybrid of rock 'n' roll crooning, early Elvis, and Iggy Pop's energetic gyration. At other shows he often performed an acoustic encore of some of his favourite Depeche Mode songs: 'I Feel You' and others. The relative success of his own record made it easier for him to go back to the band. It meant that he could insist on being allowed to write some of the songs on the next album, without having to feel awkward.

"When the time is right, Martin and I will sit down and talk," he said. "For now, I don't know about the future. I'm moving forward and I'm writing my own songs."

The success of the record also gave him a bit of a confidence boost, something he needed after having his dramatic fall from grace played out in public. He might have seemed very confident on-stage but in private he was still subject to major insecurities. "I'm a good example of somebody with an over-inflated ego but an incredibly low self-esteem," he said in an interview with a fansite, "and they really go hand in hand. It's like I'm the greatest thing since sliced bread on one hand and the lowest creature from the black lagoon that you can possibly imagine on the other side – and of course I'm neither, but somehow I found this kind of balance and I think making this album has helped me to achieve that."

# 20

# REUNION

With the interviews Dave gave to promote *Paper Monsters*, he did little to allay the fears of those who thought that his solo album meant the end of the band. He said at one point that his role in Depeche Mode was to be "an instrument used by others". This was perhaps a reference to a comment Martin had made in a previous interview. "Dave is like another instrument," he said. "He's the voice of the band. His voice is particularly suited to a lot of the songs. I can't sing the way he does." Of course Martin meant this as a compliment but this may not have been the way it sounded to Dave. By now he wasn't prepared to accept being an "instrument" anymore. He wanted to be the one playing the instrument.

For Daniel Miller, 2003 must have been a worrying time. Although he always supported his artists in whatever they wanted to do, the idea that Depeche Mode might have been breaking up would have been alarming. 2002 had been a significant year for Mute as, after fourteen years of independence, he sold the company to EMI. Like many independents, the label found life sometimes tough towards the end of the 1990s and so after the massive success of Moby's *Play* album in 2000, Miller decided it was time to do a deal while he was in a position of strength. A big part of that strength, however, was the knowledge that the next Depeche Mode album was an almost guaranteed big seller.

And, if he was worried, the band's legion of fanatical supporters were even more concerned. One German reporter asked Dave if there would ever be another Depeche Mode album and, when he obviously couldn't guarantee it, the interviewer began wailing and stamping his feet. It was a ridiculous level of pressure. But most of the interviews just served as a way of venting his feelings and letting everybody know that things needed to change.

"I'm very angry with Martin," he said in another interview. "I'd never ask him, 'Hey, Mart, couldn't we do this song part in another way?' I know what his answer would be. Unless he's open to both me and him coming into the studio with songs, I don't see there's a point in carrying on."

When these interviews got back to the rest of the band, Martin was bemused but Fletch was able to be stoical about it. He was aware that both of his bandmates used magazine articles as a way of communicating with each other. For Dave there was always an element of letting off steam. "Interviews are a kind of therapy for him," Fletch said. "What Dave says and what he thinks are two different things."

This might not have been entirely true in this case but it was certainly true that Dave would be more conciliatory later on. He was trying to change things and move things forward. Still, there must have been some tense moments between the three of them. They planned to have a meeting at the end of 2003 but that got pushed back to the beginning of 2004.

It was inevitable that, for once, the two main players of Depeche Mode had some talking to do. They had a relationship that few people in the world would really be able to understand. Perhaps only Pete Townshend and Roger Daltrey of The Who would have some idea. There was a strange mutual inter-dependence between a songwriter and a singer in the same band. They each had something that the other needed. Martin must have wished, at times, that he had Dave's confidence and stage presence, while the singer must have been envious of Martin's writing. For Dave, singing Martin's songs had always been a privilege and he'd been fulsome in his praise over the years. It was, perhaps, the songwriter's difficulties in expressing himself verbally that made him such a great songwriter. He was able to say things through his songs, and through Dave, that he couldn't say any other way.

When Dave joined the band he was always the outsider, from the other side of the tracks, as they put it, from Vince, Martin and Fletch. He was a natural group member in a way that they weren't. They'd spent their time in church or in their rooms, practising their instruments or talking about what they were going to do while Dave was out living something like a rock 'n' roll lifestyle when he was barely into his teens. There was a competitive element to their relationship, which was never acknowledged and which the demarcation of labour in Depeche Mode didn't allow for. That demarcation also meant things didn't come to a head earlier. It was always very clear to everybody in the band who did what, even if outsiders were sometimes confused.

Many bands fall apart over something as simple as publishing credits. When the rest of the band notice how much bigger the songwriter's house is than theirs, they start to think that they should be getting a bigger slice of the pie. This had never been an issue in Depeche Mode. They all appreciated that it was Martin's songs that provided the starting point.

Martin's songs had been tested in the most difficult circumstances, following the departure of Vince Clarke. They'd garnered them an eager audience of millions waiting to see what they would do next. Dave was in a position of strength in that, following his solo career, he no longer needed Depeche Mode as much as he had in the past. If he wasn't able to take a greater creative part in their albums then he could simply walk away. The answer was something that they'd never been very good at before: compromise.

Martin has numerous songs that take a dim view of compromise, albeit in the context of a relationship. In 'Stories Of Old' on '*Some Great Reward* and 'Freelove' on *Exciter*, among others, he spells out what he sees as the disastrous consequences of people allowing themselves to be diverted from their true selves in order to please somebody else.

This was true, too, of his work in Depeche Mode. He wouldn't overtly turn down other ideas. He would just carry on quietly heading in his own direction in the certain knowledge that, in the end, the rest of them would follow. When Alan decided that he didn't want to follow anymore he left. But if Dave left, he knew, it couldn't be the same band anymore. He had to make a decision, to allow the singer to write some of the songs on the next album, or accept that there wouldn't be another album at all.

While the power struggle continued, Daniel Miller put together a compilation of the many remixes that Depeche Mode had commissioned over the years. To many purist fans' horror, Mike Shinoda of Linkin Park re-mixed 'Enjoy The Silence' and it was duly released as a single. Unsurprisingly he created a paradoxically noisy version. The added clatter didn't take away from the brilliance of Dave's vocal but it did seem like an unnecessary addition to a great song. This was perhaps the period in the band's history when they were furthest away from many of their fans. They'd stood by them through Dave's drug abuse and subsequent stint in rehab. The constant squabbling in the press, though, proved highly disillusioning. The Shinoda remix was taken as a sign, perhaps unfairly, that they were no longer in touch with the devoted black-clad hordes in the way that they'd once been.

Luckily things were, at last, looking up. The main thing that brought them back together was time. There was a four year gap between the last Depeche Mode album *Exciter* and the next *Playing The Angel*. They'd had a chance to miss each other and, more importantly, miss making Depeche Mode records and playing them live. Nevertheless there were some tense moments when they met for the first time after Dave's notorious *Paper Monsters* interviews.

"During the press for his solo record, he went a bit too far, saying stuff like he felt like a puppet and I was a dictator, and he felt he had a right to contribute," Martin said to Danny Eccleston in *Mojo*. "I realised during that period that if the band were going to continue then I would have to allow that to happen up to a point. But I didn't think it was right that after 25 years he should step in and write 50 per cent of the songs." Perhaps it simply depended on how good the songs were. If Depeche Mode could carry on producing great songs, then maybe most of the fans wouldn't care who'd written them.

Essentially Dave was making the rather bold claim that his songs could be as good as those of a man who'd written albums that had sold over 50 million copies worldwide. "My guess is that he would feel that it was something being taken away from him rather than something that was being given," Dave said.

It was a lot of pressure but he did have the advantage that his songs were new and fresh. Martin had never found songwriting easy. By the time they came together to discuss the next album Dave had, according to Fletch, written 17 songs, Martin only four. Of course, as Martin occasionally liked to point out, they weren't solely "Dave's songs". He was now writing with session musicians Christian Eigner and Andrew Phillpott. Christian had been the touring drummer in Depeche Mode since 1997 while Andrew had worked on the programming for their tours as well as on Martin's album of cover versions *Counterfeit 2*. They both had a thorough understanding of how the band worked and they were able to provide the structure that Dave's demos sometimes lacked. It also helped that they understood that their role was to help make his songs as good as they could possibly be. That they were perfectly happy to be in the background is suggested by their production nom de plume "Das Shadow". There wasn't the sometime ego-clash of Depeche Mode.

Still, when Dave met Martin in Santa Barbara there was also a great deal of sympathy between them. Martin been going through his own problems. His relationship with his wife, designer Suzanne Boisvert, had crumbled during the period between the two albums and he was going through a divorce made understandably more painful by his feelings for his children. It was a situation that Dave was all too familiar with so, in their own unostentatious way, he and Fletch were able to rally round. So much had happened to them in the last few years that the problems they'd had in the band now seemed relatively trivial. Although they would still argue, it was easier to have some perspective on things.

It also helped that Fletch and Martin liked Dave's songs. Working with them provided a new challenge, which was welcome after so many albums. They appreciated his honesty as he simply played them the demos of nine new songs and asked for their opinion. "It was a bit like watching the Eurovision Song Contest," Fletch commented to Q.

Nevertheless, producer Ben Hillier found their working methods extremely bizarre. According to Dave he said that they were, "by far the weirdest band he's ever worked with." Working with Ben was different to their experiences on the two previous albums with Tim Simenon and Mark Bell because he wasn't steeped in Depeche Mode's history in the way that they'd been. He didn't come from an electronic music background and he was barely familiar with many of their albums. "He knew a few songs," said Dave, "and we had to actually get him the whole catalogue for him to listen to."

At one time this might have seemed like a disadvantage. They used to have a very distinct idea of what a Depeche Mode album sounded like and they wanted to work with people who understood that vision. This time, though, they were all looking for a change. They'd made enough music now that there was no point simply repeating what they'd done before. When Ben arrived they were surprised that, although he'd rarely worked with electronic bands in the past, he was a big fan of electronic music. He turned up at the studio with a collection of retro, analogue synthesisers. It must have been a little bizarre for the band that the kind of instruments they'd used when they were starting out were now sought-after museum pieces but it would give the record a very different texture. The combination of old and new technology helped give it the feel of an updated version of the old, Berlin Depeche Mode.

As Dave had suggested, the addition of a competitive element in the band did seem to spur Martin on. When they arrived at Santa Barbara in January 2005 to start work on the album, they had an unprecedented eleven songs ready to start work on.

They were worried, initially, that they wouldn't be able to fall back into the group mentality that easily again. Since they'd last been together, they'd all been working on their own projects, Dave and Martin with solo albums and Fletch with his record label Toast Hawaii. They were very aware that, in any successful band, there are powerful egos. They'd learned though, to tread carefully with each other. They recorded the album in Santa Barbara, New York and London in order that all three members could get to see their families while they were working. It was almost a surprise to find that they were getting on better than they had before. "Actually it's been very enjoyable," Martin said of the making of the album, "perhaps one of the most enjoyable since probably *Violator* or pre-*Violator*."

It helped that Dave was more enthusiastic and involved than ever. He'd got the greater creative say in areas beyond his vocals that he'd wanted, and this made for a happier experience for all of them. They also gave a lot of credit to their young producer Ben Hillier. He had strong ideas of how they should sound and they were happy to listen to what he had to say. They were looking for – to use their own words – "a headteacher".

One job they gave Ben was choosing which songs should go on the record. They'd already agreed that three of them would be Dave's and the rest Martin's so it was simply a question of deciding which worked best together. It could have been a source of acrimony but because Dave knew better than anybody what a Depeche Mode song sounds like, his tracks dovetailed neatly with Martin's.

Having worked separately, they were better able to appreciate the advantages that came from having the rest of the group to fall back on. Almost as much as being able to contribute his own songs Dave wanted to feel like they were working as a team on all the tracks. One of the songs he enjoyed most, he said, was 'John The Revelator' because they were all able to be part of it from the ground up.

It was loosely based on the traditional gospel, blues song of the same name and it was Martin's most explicit nod towards religion yet. It also emphasised the interest in blues that he and Dave had followed ever since the *Violator* sessions. The most famous version of the song, recorded by Blind Willie Johnson in 1930, included lyrics about the *Book Of Revelations* and other parts of Christian theology. Martin's lyric seemed to turn that on its head, damning those who use religion as a source of power.

When they listened to Martin developing the demo, it was changing all the time. They then added drums from Ben Hillier and Dave gave one of his classic, raw, live vocal performances on the top. It was interesting that he and Martin seemed to share a desire to give their work the patina of 'authenticity', which they'd been slightly wary of in the past. There was nothing more 'authentic' than the blues and yet theirs was an updated, modern take on the idiom.

With this latest album – *Playing The Angel* – they'd found a new energy, which Dave felt had been missing on *Exciter*. One of the things he liked about working with Ben Hillier was how fast the producer operated, not giving them time for any of the politics that had dogged them in the past. "He's great at breaking down the shit that forms between family members," Dave said to Dan Cairns in *The Sunday Times*. "Seeing very quickly the sort of roles we had devised for ourselves and going, 'This is ridiculous.' We wanted to have somebody who was that headmaster-type figure. But he was like the art teacher — you know, the one who would let you into the storeroom to bum a cigarette."

Dave had always found the long weeks or months in the studio hard to take. His dream during the *Songs Of Faith And Devotion* sessions had been of a record bashed out with raw energy and spontaneity. The kind of music Depeche Mode make often meant that this was impossible but at least with Ben, a rock producer at heart, there was a new energy to the sessions.

Despite the improvement in inter-band relations, it was evident on *Playing The Angel* that Dave had not entirely put his experiences of the mid-1990s behind him. One song, 'Suffer Well', contained a fairly overt message to his band-mates and it was a testament to Martin's tolerance that they let him put it on the album. "It was definitely a little dig at them," he said to Danny Eccleston. "I didn't write it like that but when I sang it, I did picture Martin. It was, 'Why didn't you understand that I needed you the most then?' 'Where was the fuckin' answers when I needed them most?' When I finally hit a wall, of crawling across the floor of that apartment in Santa Monica, I felt myself dying. I felt my soul had gone and inside I was screaming, 'Where the fuck are you?!'"

The title was a reference to Dave's belief that his experiences in LA had proved one thing – he was good at pain. Part of his psyche always seemed to want to test himself, see how much he could take, whether that was more than ten hours under the tattooist's needle or his notorious piercing. One of his tattoos was a Celtic dagger that he'd had done on his arm. He said that it was a way of saying that, by injecting heroin, he was essentially just stabbing himself.

"I have a man I go to see in New York," he said, "he's very wise and very old and he said to me, 'So, David, have you finished suffering?' And I say, 'I'm not sure, what do you think?' And he says, 'You only suffer as long as you want to.' I thought that was very wise."

Another of his songs on the album, 'Nothing's Impossible', could be taken either as a comment on a relationship or the relationships within the band. The central message of the title, at least, was one of optimism even though there was only the barest glimmer of light in the song's dark, moody atmosphere. He sings it with a kind of slow, doleful cadence that's incongruously at odds with the song's message.

The third of his songs, 'I Want It All', was another lyric that seemed to look back at his past problems and his tendency to feel that enough was never enough. It's striking, though, how difficult it is to distinguish Dave's songs from Martin's on *Playing The Angel*. Perhaps because they'd been through so many similar experiences, or because he'd been influenced by Martin, he had a very similar aesthetic. They were both in the mood to unburden themselves and confess. The single, 'Precious', is about Martin's children and the impact of his divorce on them. The fact that Dave, who could relate to the lyric only too well, sings Martin's words is highly affecting. It showed that there was still room in Depeche Mode for the unique partnership between the two of them.

On a German interview after the release of the album, Dave admitted: "We didn't know what it was going to be like when we got together but after the first few weeks we really got into it. We weren't sure how it was going to be until we actually got in and started working together. Once we got in the studio it always becomes the Depeche Mode thing."

Sonically *Playing The Angel* was an interesting departure from everything they'd done in the past. It had certain echoes of the industrial sounds of their Berlin period but they were much less grandiose. It's a minor key album. It sounds like it was recorded in some deep cavern below the ground. It's rather lacking in hooks and yet it has a powerful and moving atmosphere. It seems to look back over their career, with some synth sounds, on 'Damaged People', for example, that they wouldn't have used since *Speak And Spell*.

It was a combination of sounds and styles that enthused fans who were disappointed by *Exciter*'s more laid-back groove. On the back they put the legend, "pain and suffering in various tempos". It was a joke that referred not just to that album but to their career as a whole. It put to bed much of what they'd been through in the last few years. The frequent references to angels and Dave's 'Suffer Well' seemed to refer to overcoming problems and getting through them.

There were still inevitably clashes between the different members of the band. Martin remembered a typically ludicrous bust-up when they were making the video for 'Precious'. Director Uwe Fläder was explaining the idea behind the video to them, that they would be playing in a kind of sci-fi ballroom and Dave suggested that Andy should play the piano. Andy suggested that it might be better if he played an old synth and, as Martin recalled to *Mojo,* Dave stormed out raging: "Well, I only want what's best for the band!" Not long afterwards he was back, apologetic, but it was a sign of the kind of tensions that still bubbled under the surface. In Depeche Mode's career there had been innumerable bust-ups between all of them but their strength had been their ability to keep going regardless.

When 'Precious' was released, it went some way to reassuring them all. It wasn't an obvious pop single. It had one of Martin's most moving lyrics and a beautiful melody but the chorus was subtle and elusive. They hadn't released any original music for three years and, as always, they wondered whether people were still interested. They undoubtedly were. It went straight in to Number 4 in the UK charts.

The release, in October 2005, of *Playing The Angel* seemed to demonstrate that if they'd successfully moved on, then the fans had moved on with them too. It would eventually go on to sell more than three and a half million copies. It went to Number 1 in an astonishing 17 countries. Even in the cynical UK and USA, they went Top Ten. This was despite most reviews saying, essentially, that it was a good album but not one that anybody except 'real' fans would ever care about. "If you really are the sort of person who's been waiting with bated breath for a new Depeche Mode release, then don't worry: You'll love this," said influential website *Pitchfork*. "Dear everyone else: It's pretty okay."

As so often, many of their positive reviews had a slightly surprised tone, as though the writer had listened to them for the first time in years and was amazed to discover that they were still pretty good. There was also a widespread assumption that they were trying to be dark and that the tunes arrived almost by default.

"Their dark nights of the soul always produce the shiniest melodies," said *The Guardian*, "rather than the Nick Cave-ish atonality they probably strive for." They were back to where they'd been circa *Music For The Masses*, of interest only to 'real' fans but, lucky for them, they had an awful lot of real fans.

After it was released Martin said he had fans come up to him and tell him that they knew it was the last Depeche Mode album. He was surprised. He had no intention of stopping there, but you can see what they meant. There's something strangely final about it. It seems to draw a line under everything they'd done before.

Perhaps, in a way, it did. Dave said that the three songs he'd been able to contribute this time were "just a start". It promised more of the kind of awkward confrontation that they'd never been very good at, in the future. For now, though, there was a new equilibrium within the band that seemed to be holding. The next singles 'A Pain That I'm Used To', 'Suffer Well' and 'John The Revelator' all fitted neatly into the remarkably consistent pattern of singles throughout their career. They were the consummate Top 20 band. They joked once that if they ever actually had a Number 1 then it would all be over.

'Suffer Well', which saw Anton's video return, was a sort of four-minute trip through Dave's decline and fall, with a memorable appearance from Martin and Fletch as shop dummies representing a bride and groom respectively. What Anton was able to do was provide a simple plot that would keep you watching even if you didn't like the song. The video also saw Dave "acting" even more than he had in the past as he changed from a suave-suited lover to a desperate tramp and back again.

Then in March 2006 the band offered perhaps their most bizarre version of one of their songs, Dave's 'Suffer Well', recorded in "Simlish", the language of computer game *The Sims*. "Depeche Mode has always been open to new ways of sharing our music," said Dave when it was announced. "But re-recording a Simlish-language version of 'Suffer Well' just sounded bizarre. Of course, that's why we couldn't resist doing it."

Perhaps unsurprisingly Dave sounds a little embarrassed singing in "Simlish" (supposedly a mixture of Ukrainian and the Filipino language Tagalog). The executive behind *The Sims*, Steve Schnur, described Simlish as "an emotion-filled language that defies translation. It's a great fit for the music of Depeche Mode which is so focused on creating a mood and appeals to people on an emotional level." In reality it sounded like they'd played his normal singing backwards. However, it did come with a rather excellent tragi-comic video featuring a Sim robot falling in love with a Sim woman.

By 2006, it was a good time to look back and in that year they began a series of reissues of all Depeche Mode albums, starting with *Speak And Spell*. As part of the process they also recorded a documentary for each one and, for Dave, it was an interesting but also slightly disturbing opportunity to listen to his juvenilia. He barely ever listened to any of their albums when they were finished, only *Violator* and *Songs Of Faith And Devotion* occasionally. More disturbing, though, was some of the archive footage of what they used to look like back then. "It's kind of horrifying, seeing some of it," Dave said in a TV interview, "but it means I've got a diary now of stuff that I'd completely forgotten about."

There were also some proud moments, particularly talking about *Violator*, which he now recognised as a career peak. "I can see why that record took us to a new place," he said. "We were experimenting with blues and gospel and mixing it with electronica and it was an interesting combination."

With their confidence restored, *Touring The Angel* once again saw them heading out on the kind of mammoth trek that they'd done in the past. It was 78 dates, nothing compared to *Music For The Masses* but still a sizeable chunk of their lives. However, things were very different. "On tour now, or definitely the last two tours, I wake up and remember everything that happened the night before!" Dave said to the *Manchester Evening News*. "I remember people's faces in the audience and I remember the way it felt, and I want to do that again and that's my drive."

But ironically *Touring The Angel* seemed to be cursed with more bad luck than some of their previous, more debauched tours. Along the way they ran into hurricanes, sickness, problems with promoters and a cancelled date due to war in Lebanon.

The first date in Fort Lauderdale had to be cancelled due to Hurricane Wilma sweeping through Florida. Instead they began in Tampa further inland with an Anton Corbijn-designed set that was their most futuristic yet. At one side of the stage was a giant ball on which was painted some classic Depeche Mode song themes: "sex", "pain" etc. Above was a massive image of the alien creature on the front of the record sleeve and on either side were sci-fi style pods from which they played.

The summer leg of the tour, dubbed the 'Open Air' tour because most of the gigs were outdoors, was even bigger but that too started inauspiciously. Halfway through the show Dave started faltering. He was clearly struggling to sing as well as normal and in the end he walked off. Martin attempted to make up for it with an acoustic performance but the fans, understandably, weren't happy. Boos rang out as Fletch haltingly apologised and said, "Thanks for coming to support us," before he glumly walked off the stage.

There were all kinds of rumours initially, that Dave was upset with the sound engineers and that they'd just had some kind of tantrum after technical problems. This was obviously highly implausible and incorrect. After hundreds of dates in all kinds of situations around the world, they would hardly abandon a show in front of thousands of people because of a few minor sound problems. It was only when they had to cancel the next night's show, in Chicago, that the official explanation – Dave had laryngitis and couldn't physically sing – was announced. It must have seemed strangely ironic that they'd managed to get through the gigantic *Devotional* tour with only two cancelled shows, and yet, here they were, losing one and a half already.

Later on they had to cancel another date, in Lisbon, because of issues with a promoter and, finally, they had to cancel their first ever show in Israel because of the conflict with Lebanon.

Depeche Mode then announced Martin had written fourteen songs and that they were looking to go into the studio as soon as Dave had finished his next solo album. The last date of the tour was in Athens, Greece and that was particularly significant for Dave because of his wife Jennifer's Greek origins. The whole family came out for it and initially he was very conscious of the fact that they were watching him.

"My mother and my wife's mother were at the side of the stage," he said in an interview with Greek TV, "and I kept thinking that I have to be careful because my mother-in-law's watching me! I shouldn't get too down and dirty with my performance but then I thought halfway through that I've got to do my thing."

Despite its problems, the tour confirmed their position as one of the few bands who were genuinely worth seeing in an arena. They had songs that didn't need to be experienced at close quarters to be effective and the communal experience enhanced rather than diminished them. "Despite their tinny, synth-pop origins," said *The Times*, "the veteran group from Basildon have long since morphed into one of the most powerful and consistently enthralling arena-rock attractions." They had so many songs now that the only criticism from some fans was that they played too many singles and not enough cult hits. It was interesting to note which albums were now in favour. Often they'd play nothing from *Some Great Reward,* and *A Broken Frame* was almost totally ignored.

When they came to release another *Best Of* in 2006, though, they produced a more inclusive version of their history. It included tracks from every album except *Black Celebration*, the one, famously, with "no singles". It also included an excellent new track 'Martyr' which had originally been intended for *Playing The Angel,* but they decided that it was too poppy to find a place among the dark, bluesy electronica of that album. It was a fair point because 'Martyr' was like a throwback to an earlier era, the hyped-up, dark party music of 'Strangelove' or 'Master And Servant'.

They'd succeeded in rejuvenating themselves and Dave Gahan's solo career, far from destroying them, seemed to have made them stronger. Just as he'd said so many years before, though, Dave still couldn't "get enough". Indeed 'I Want It All' on *Playing The Angel* had made exactly the same point. Writing songs and making music now constantly whet his appetite. Not long after finishing with *Playing The Angel,* he was off to make another David Gahan solo album.

# 21

# HOURGLASS

After *Touring The Angel*, Dave had just a month at home before he was quickly itching to do something else. There was always a period of adjustment after coming off tour: "It's always quite difficult after a tour," he said. "You're kind of waiting for somebody to put a note under your door with what it is you've got to do that day. You create new obsessions, like how to load the dishwasher correctly and stuff like that."

He was learning, he said in a Q+A session with fans, that he couldn't take his work home with him. "You get to feel a lot of emotions," he explained, "and they're all mixed up because you're getting in touch with who you are. When I go home it's immediately grounding to be around my family, especially my young daughter. It doesn't take very long at all for her to do a couple of cartwheels in front of me and I realise what's really important."

His wife, Jennifer, was also capable of reminding him that he wasn't a rock star when he was at home. "'You can't act like that round here,' gets said a lot," he admitted. It was the kind of grounding that he'd always needed but that, in the past, he hadn't always been ready to appreciate.

As he had for his songs on *Playing The Angel*, he called up Andrew Phillpott and Christian Eigner and suggested they go into his studio in New York. It was on one of the city's busiest streets and the constant noise outside appealed to him, just as it had when he was making *Paper Monsters*.

Initially it wasn't clear that they were making another solo album. They just started working on the demos that he'd come up with, playing around amidst the clouds of all three members' constant cigarette smoke. As he'd written many songs that hadn't gone on *Playing The Angel*, there was no shortage of material. It was also a liberating experience to work so quickly without the technical deliberation of Depeche Mode's studio work. On one track, 'Deeper And Deeper', he only delivered a couple of rough, raw vocal takes because the way he was singing was so punishing on his vocal chords. "I'm pushing my vocals to the limit on that one," he said in a TV interview. "After a couple of takes it was done, not because it was 'good enough' but because that was it. My voice was done."

On another track, 'Endless' the energy of the city literally became part of the record. They left it so that they could hear the sounds of traffic outside, including the siren of a passing police car. They'd decided to produce the record themselves and that, too, gave it a kind of rough-and-ready quality that Dave appreciated.

After two or three weeks they were saying to each other "this sounds like a record" he said. He called up Daniel Miller to come and listen and he was encouraged by the response. "He was like 'Carry on'", Dave said in a TV interview afterwards. "He gave us the thumbs up and I didn't get the thumbs up with *Paper Monsters*, it was more like, 'Interesting, you need to write a little more!'"

If Daniel had been concerned during *Paper Monsters* that Depeche Mode might fall apart, he was now reasonably confident that the worst of their interpersonal problems were over. When he heard a record that was so Mode-esque he was delighted to be able to put it out. It had an obvious appeal to at least some of the millions of the fans who'd bought *Playing The Angel*.

They were able to get a glimpse of Dave's working methods in a series of video clips from the $11^{th}$ floor Studio that he posted up on Youtube. Essentially they made working on a Dave Gahan album look like a science lesson in which one of the kids (Dave, obviously) is distracting the other two, messing around and enjoying himself. The actual music, just about audible in the background, was starkly different. It was an object lesson that dark, serious tunes can come out of a light-hearted, cheerful atmosphere.

And if *Paper Monsters* had come out of Dave's desire to be part of a band, this was more like the Depeche Mode record that could have been. The rock elements were reduced in favour of an electronic sound that was very reminiscent of his day-job. Admittedly Depeche Mode would never have a guitar solo like the one on 'Saw Something'. It was provided by another rock legend and former heroin addict, the Red Hot Chili Pepper's John

## DEPECHE MODE & THE SECOND COMING

Frusciante. However, it's the only moment on the album that it's impossible to imagine Martin Gore countenancing.

The album's first single, 'Kingdom', was sleek, dark electronica with perhaps only slightly more of a nod to U2 than Martin would have allowed. The other difference was that a Dave Gahan solo project didn't have the weight of expectation of Depeche Mode albums. It was a relief to be working on something without the pressure of 25 years of massive success.

"Immediately people start going, 'Okay, do we hear a single? Will it get played on the radio?'" he said of Depeche Mode's recording sessions. "All that stuff, to me, is becoming really not that important anymore."

Instead, the second solo album – *Hourglass* – seems to be an exercise in what Depeche Mode would be like if Dave was in the driving seat. The answer, perhaps surprisingly, was not all that different. If anything it was further proof of how close he and Martin were in terms of their lyrical themes, love of bluesy electronica and dark beats.

The differences on the album, then, are harder to spot than the similarities. Perhaps there's a slightly more American tone. 'Deeper And Deeper', for example, with its gravelly vocal, was a nod towards bands like Nine Inch Nails who'd been influenced by the darker side of Depeche Mode. This was also true of 'Use You', with its whipcrack beats and cynical lyric. These were both tracks that represented the character he'd described as "evil Dave" in interviews for *Paper Monsters*. Although Martin had written his fair share of dark songs, he'd never written anything as explicitly malevolent as 'Deeper And Deeper'. Like Martin, though, there was also an element to the album that was far more spiritual. '21 Days' was gospel of the kind that had appeared on his favourite album, *Songs Of Faith And Devotion,* while 'Miracles' had even more explicit broodings on religion.

The one thing that the album perhaps lacked was the kind of hooks that had made Depeche Mode multi-million unit shifting megastars in the first place. Instead of vibrant choruses it had atmosphere and groove. It was the kind of record to be listened to late at night, rather than in a club or before going out. The production of Andrew Phillpott and Christian Eigner provided a dark backdrop for Dave to exercise all his vocal tricks. From the enthusiastic kid of *Speak And Spell* to the bruised troubadour of *Ultra*, he'd learned all manner of ways of expressing himself. If it wasn't as essential as the best Depeche Mode records, it was still another great outing for one of the best voices in pop.

The whole process of writing, recording and producing the album took just eight weeks. That, in itself, was a relief after the extended sessions he had with Depeche Mode. There was no politics because he was in charge in a way that was not possible within the delicate equilibrium of a pop group. The title *Hourglass* initially seemed to be a reference to time running out.

"Something about living in New York pushes the clock as well," he told *NME*. "Once the city's awake it never really sleeps. But I wanted to slow down and accept that that's where I'm at. Time is looming for me. But it's OK. I don't wanna waste anymore time sitting around thinking about it. I wanna be out there doing things that are creative."

He was certainly working now as though he needed to produce music as quickly as he could. In the same interview, though, he also pointed out that the great thing about hourglasses is that you can always turn them over and start again. By 2007 he'd been clean for over ten years. When he was asked during the promotion of *Hourglass* if he'd remain clean he was able to say, "I think so, thank God. But I still have the same feelings of wanting to escape, of wanting to be somewhere else. But now I'm very aware that those crutches don't work anymore." He had reached a place of serenity at last.

When the reviews came in for *Hourglass,* Dave was startled at how good they were. Only the inevitable comparisons with Martin's songs irked him slightly. "Dave Gahan's second solo outing is reliably bleak," said *The Guardian*, "probing the murk of his post-heroin-addiction mind as you'd expect, but achieving a kind of magnificence, too." Many critics saw it as a kind of challenge to Martin, as though he was trying to prove that he could write just as good Depeche Mode songs. *The Times* described it as a, "solo album that sounds like a Depeche Mode album. Gahan does Gore. And not at all badly – 'Kingdom' is stronger than anything the Mode have done recently. So, is the power struggle intensifying? Mode fans will like *Hourglass*; Gore, not so much."

This was unfair. Throughout the recording of *Hourglass*, both Martin and Dave were clear that there was going to be another Depeche Mode album. Martin had already started writing songs and they were in communication about the next recording sessions.

"Martin had some really encouraging words for me," Dave said in a TV interview. "I sent him a copy of *Hourglass* of course and he told me to tell people that it was his album of the year! Which was nice, coming from Martin." Dave had so often spoken in interviews about his wish that his band-mate would be more encouraging, but there's no reason to doubt that Martin enjoyed his new direction. Why wouldn't he? It was far closer to the kind of music that he was into than *Paper Monsters* had been.

Dave played a few shows to support the record but when asked if he'd be touring it he was blunt in his response. Having not long since come off a seven month Depeche Mode tour, he wouldn't be doing that again. He had his family.

When *Hourglass* was released in October 2007 then, there was no chance that it was going to reach the commercial heights of his work with the band. Nevertheless it demonstrated his enduring popularity in Germany, reaching Number 2. Elsewhere it did less well, not even going Top 40 in the UK. He did, however, have a surprise Number 1 hit in Spain with 'Kingdom'. It wasn't such an enormous seller to threaten the existence of Depeche Mode but it proved that Dave wasn't deluding himself as a songwriter. And, in 2008, as he was about to start recording another album with Martin, that was the most important thing of all.

## 22

# AROUND THE UNIVERSE

While promoting *Hourglass*, Dave also announced that Depeche Mode were going back into the studio. Martin was writing songs in Santa Barbara and, in March 2008, they went to his house in California for a meeting. It was much less fraught than the one they'd had four years previously. They'd all reached the point where they realised how lucky they were to still be making records after all these years. "I'm still pinching myself," Dave said in a TV interview, "still waiting for somebody to tap me on the shoulder and say, 'Time to dig some ditches now.'"

In May 2008 Depeche Mode went back into the studio. The clean atmosphere created a kind of camaraderie between Martin and the frontman that they'd very rarely had before. They'd always managed to concentrate on the music, even at the peak of their excess, but now that there was nothing else to do in the studio, a new addiction emerged. Martin had started collecting vintage synths that he found on the internet and that soon became something of an obsession!

The recording of the new album took place in an environment that was something between a toy shop and a 1960s sci-fi film. They were "playing" in both senses and they tried to capture some of the new light-hearted spirit with a series of wobbly, Fletch-shot videos posted on Youtube. These seemed to suggest that recording in Depeche Mode was more fun than it had ever been. One memorable moment had Martin delivering his vocal into a plastic bottle. Another saw Dave limbering up his vocal chords with a quick Elvis impression. The whole process looked strangely home-made, analogue and rickety. It wasn't just blokes sitting in front of laptops as Dave had complained in the past. Martin's guitar was very much in evidence as well as various strange bits of antiquated synth technology. They were once asked if it was harder to make emotional music with new technology. The answer was evidently that, although they might have been using state of the art computers, there was still a place for synths they'd have laughed at in 1981.

For the first time Martin and Dave even co-wrote a song, even if it wasn't exactly Paul McCartney and John Lennon in 1963. Martin wrote an instrumental and then Dave took it away to add a melody and some lyrics. The song, apparently inspired by a toe-stubbing incident during a game of table football was, perhaps, not the most serious thing they'd ever written but it was a sign of a new mellowness in their relationship. As they jammed and messed around, they looked very much like a band, albeit an extremely bizarre one. There were undoubtedly arguments as well. Yet in reality there had always been good times to go along with the more widely publicised spats. They might have regarded Depeche Mode as a job they had to do every four years but this was not for the money anymore. However frustrating and infuriating it could be, it was a part of their identities.

After a few weeks they had far more songs than they could put on one album. That could easily have led to more arguments. Instead there was a mutual understanding that Martin was the main songwriter but that Dave had earned his right to at least three songs on the album. It was noticeable, once again, how close their writing style had become.

Within Depeche Mode, Dave had finally found the kind of strongly defined role, as singer, frontman and songwriter that he'd always craved. Somehow, he was able to negotiate a new, broader role for himself and the rest of the band ultimately accepted that. For a group who managed to function for years while saying as little as possible to each other about how they felt, it was quite a turnaround.

Part of their success, though, had been a refusal to be satisfied. Although they all agreed that everything they'd done after *Some Great Reward* had been worthwhile, there were still areas where they thought they could improve. They also had a streak of insecurity and pessimism, which, while it caused them certain problems, always kept them on their toes.

"Fletch and Martin didn't give up their jobs for the first couple of years and we're still pretty pessimistic," Dave once joked. It's not hard to see why. Right from the start they seemed like a band who were about to collapse. Dave and Martin's association was entirely based on musical ability. It was slightly absurd that two such different people had found themselves tied together for almost thirty years. Nevertheless they had earned each other's respect. "We don't sit around giving each other hugs," Dave said, "but I think deep down we all love and respect each other."

On October 6, 2008, Depeche Mode held a press conference in Berlin. They'd got a little bit better at this sort of thing than at the awkward occasion in the Rose Bowl some twenty years before, but not much. Wearing all black and looking like kids trying to remember their lines at a school play, they sat in front of an invited crowd and a large number of photographers and announced the start of a new tour dubbed, *The Tour Of The Universe*. Fittingly the tour would start in Tel Aviv, scene of their cancelled gig on the previous jaunt.

As they answered questions, they slowly began to look more relaxed. When Fletch reassured fans that morale in the camp was extremely high, there was no reason to doubt it. Even when a journalist asked how many songs Dave had written for the new album, there was only a flicker of tension on his and Martin's faces. This evidently hadn't been decided for certain but his answer, that they'd recorded two and were "probably" going to do two more, suggested there was still some negotiating to come. "Martin's written some fantastic songs," he said, "and this is the first time we've had when it's going to be difficult to choose the album."

At that point they weren't prepared to release the name of the album but Martin did reveal that old friend Daryl Bamonte had heard it and joked, "It's about time you had another really arrogant title.'" "That's it," Martin said, "it was sealed."

But there was obviously a clue in the name of the tour. As Fletch joked: "We've been told by some important people in the US military that we will be finding life on other planets so we want to be the first group to go there." That was with one of the easier questions that they had to deal with. As they responded to queries about what songs they were going to play, whether Anton Corbijn would be designing the stage sets and whether there would be more dates added at the end, they seemed to realise that things were still

## DEPECHE MODE & THE SECOND COMING

very much up in the air. "We're announcing it without really knowing what we're gonna do!" said Martin.

They didn't look too unhappy about this. When asked why they'd kept on going for so many years, Martin answered that it was simply because they didn't know what to expect. Their whole career had been one of surprises, not all of them pleasant, but the main one was that they were still around.

By now the band frequently referred to Depeche Mode as "a marriage". Obviously this wasn't entirely a compliment. Dave had been divorced twice and Martin once. Still, there was no question that the band could have got "divorced" if they'd wanted to but they'd chosen not to. They'd moved on and things had even become much better than they'd been for many years.

"With these last two albums I feel that I'm growing again as a musician, with my voice and writing songs," said Dave after the recording of *Sounds Of The Universe*. "I feel much more comfortable with my position in the band. It's taken several years."

The response to the press conference was astonishing. Despite the fact that fans had yet to hear any of the new music, and that these dates weren't for another eight months, the tickets sold out almost immediately. In London a spokesperson for the 02 Arena said that tickets "sold out in literally minutes, blocking phone lines and crashing websites as fans scrambled for tickets, all European promoters are reporting record sales with early sell outs across mainland Europe." Their previous tour, *Playing The Angel*, sold 1.8 million tickets and it seemed like, if anything, Depeche Mode might be even bigger now.

The album received its first unofficial exposure when a track, 'Fragile Tension', was leaked on to the internet in early February 2009. It was just a rough demo, they said, but interest was already mounting. On February 21, 2009 the first single 'Wrong' had its premier at Germany's Echo Awards Ceremony in Berlin. For the next two days the film of their performance was the most popular clip on Youtube. 'Wrong' seemed to hark back to the poppiest moments of their mid-period. It was a deceptively simple song with an unforgettable central hook and it seemed closer to 'Martyr' than anything on their previous album. It was very much of the Depeche Mode formula, a dark central subject delivered with uplifting energy. But, by now, that formula allowed for so much experimentation and diversity that it was hard to know what they would come up with.

Finally, on April 20, 2009, the twelfth Depeche Mode album – *Sounds Of The Universe* – was released. Confirming their continuing global popularity, it went Top Three in thirty countries and Number 1 in twenty countries. It was also enthusiastically received by most critics. As a band who'd made their name as innovators they were, in some ways, in a more difficult position than many groups. It wasn't enough to just keep churning out the same sounds. Fans expected something different every time. For now, though, they'd managed it and they were already promising to come back in three years time.

On May 9, 2009, Dave Gahan was 47 years old. The next day he went to Tel Aviv in Israel to start yet another major tour around the world. Having been forced to cancel their last gig there, they were desperate to make it up to the 50,000 fans who'd bought tickets. However, there was to be yet another twist. Dave was starting to feel ill. It wasn't yet bad enough to make him think about cancelling. How could they cancel such an enormous gig for the second time? Two days later, though, in Greece, his problems had gone beyond just an upset stomach. He was taken to hospital and diagnosed with severe gastroenteritis. For many former drug-using rock stars, this kind of thing comes with its own additional negative rumours. For Dave Gahan, however, his drug use was so far back in his distant past that no one considered it as a possibility. He had clearly conquered that demon.

When the tests results finally came back, however, it was dreadful news – doctors had found a tumour in his bladder. This surely meant the end of the tour. Although, somewhat reassuringly, it was described as a "low grade" malignant tumour, it seemed unlikely that he would simply get back on stage immediately after surgery to remove it.

*Incredibly*, that's exactly what the band did. On June 8 in Leipzig, Germany they were able to restart the tour. They also announced even more dates, stretching right through to February 2010. It was an astonishingly ambitious schedule for somebody who'd just recovered from surgery. It also showed the global scale of their

# DEPECHE MODE & THE SECOND COMING

following, they'd be playing everywhere from Bogota in Colombia to Budapest in Hungary.

In 2009, despite his not inconsiderable health worries, Dave Gahan sang to over two million people, moving them in a way that the fresh-faced pop star who sang 'Just Can't Get Enough' would barely have believed. He once described Depeche Mode's music as "head" music and said that his role was to provide the heartbeat. For all his mistakes that's what he's done consistently, even in his lowest moments, for years. Even after the heart, literally, stopped beating.

There's no other band as big as Depeche Mode that has such loyal fans but it's not a blind loyalty. They recognise in the three boys from Basildon a common touch that few other stars have retained and part of that is the sheer joy that Dave Gahan radiates on stage. He still appreciates his fans and the success that they've brought, despite having experienced it for almost thirty years.

There aren't many working-class lads made good still making great records twenty-plus years into their career, so we should appreciate Dave Gahan for that. By the close of the band's next tour, no doubt, Dave Gahan will be aching and wondering why he's still jumping up and down on stage every night. At the end of every show, though, the worldwide community of Depeche Mode fans will be confidently making arrangements to see them again in 2013 … and beyond.

This story probably isn't the way Dave Gahan thought his career would pan out in 1980, or, for that matter, in 1985, 1995, or even 2003. The fragile equilibrium of both Depeche Mode and his own personal life has threatened to fall apart on numerous occasions. Somehow, though, they've carried on going and he has made it through. Both Depeche Mode and Dave Gahan have made a career out of comebacks.

Dave's biggest comeback, in 1996, now seems like a million years ago. If he hadn't made it, Depeche Mode's posthumous legend might be writ large in popular culture. His face would be on t-shirts, forever strangely deified as yet another 'iconic' rock casualty. As it is, his life has served as a lesson in how much better it is to *keep on going*. For all his anxiety that his fans – and most worryingly for him as a father, his children – might see his life as

## DAVE GAHAN

a glorification of the rock 'n' roll myth, his tale is in fact the exact opposite of that. The choice between burning out and fading away, as the song has it, was always a false one. Dave Gahan is the living proof of that.

# DEPECHE MODE & DAVE GAHAN UK DISCOGRAPHY

## STUDIO ALBUMS

**Speak And Spell**: *New Life / I Sometimes Wish I Was Dead / Puppets / Boys Say Go! / No disco / What's Your Name / Photographic / Tora! Tora! Tora! / Big Muff / Any Second Now (Voices) / Just Can't Get Enough*
Mute 1981

**A Broken Frame**: *Leave In Silence / My Secret Garden / Monument / Nothing To Fear / See You / Satellite / The Meaning Of Love / A Photograph Of You / Shouldn't Have Done That / The Sun & The Rainfall*
Mute 1982

**Construction Time Again**: *Love, In Itself / More Than A Party / Pipeline / Everything Counts / Two Minute Warning / Shame / The Landscape Is Changing / Told You So / And Then... / Everything Counts (Reprise)*
Mute 1983

**Some Great Reward**: *Something To Do / Lie To Me / People Are People / It Doesn't Matter / Stories Of Old / Somebody / Master And Servant / If You Want / Blasphemous Rumours*
Mute 1984

**Black Celebration**: *Black Celebration / Fly On The Windscreen / A Question Of Lust / Sometimes / It Doesn't Matter Two / A Question Of Time / Stripped / Here Is The House / World Full Of Nothing / Dressed In Black / New Dress*
Mute 1986

**Music For The Masses**: *Never Let Me Down Again / The Things You Said / Strangelove / Sacred / Little 15 / Behind The Wheel / I Want You Now / To Have And To Hold / Nothing / Pimpf / Interlude #1 – Mission Impossible*
Mute 1988

**Violator**: *World In My Eyes / Sweetest Perfection / Personal Jesus / Halo / Waiting For The Night / Enjoy The Silence / Interlude #2 – Crucified / Policy Of Truth / Blue Dress / Interlude #3 / Clean*
Mute 1990

**Songs Of Faith And Devotion**: *I Feel You / Walking In My Shoes / Condemnation / Mercy In You / Judas / In Your Room / Get Right With Me /*

*Interlude #4 / Rush / One Caress / Higher Love*
Mute 1993

**Ultra**: *Barrel Of A Gun / The Love Thieves / Home / It's No Good / Uselink / Useless / Sister Of Night / Jazz Thieves / Freestate / The Bottom Line / Insight / Junior Painkiller*
Mute 1997

**Exciter**: *Dream On / Shine / The Sweetest Condition / When The Body Speaks / The Dead Of Night / Lovetheme / Freelove / Comatose / I Feel Loved / Breathe / Easy Tiger / I Am You / Goodnight Lovers*
Mute 2001

**Playing The Angel**: *A Pain That I'm Used To / John The Revelator / Suffer Well / The Sinner In Me / Precious / Macro / I Want It All / Nothing's Impossible / Introspectre / Damaged People / Lilian / The Darkest Star*
Mute 2007

**Sounds Of The Universe**: *In Chains / Hole To Feed / Wrong / Fragile Tension / Little Soul / In Sympathy / Peace / Come Back / Spacewalker / Perfect / Miles Away / The Truth Is / Jezebel / Corrupt*
Mute 2009

## COMPILATION ALBUMS

**The Singles 81>85**: *Dreaming Of Me / New Life / Just Can't Get Enough / See You / Leave In Silence / Get The Balance Right / Everything Counts / Love In Itself / People Are People / Master And Servant / Blasphemous Rumours / Shake The Disease / It's Called A Heart*
Mute 1985

**101**: Disc 1: *Pimpf / Behind The Wheel / Strangelove / Something To Do / Blasphemous Rumours / Stripped / Somebody / The Things You Said / Black Celebration* Disc 2: *Shake The Disease / Pleasure, Little Treasure / People Are People / A Question Of Time / Never Let Me Down Again / Master And Servant / Just Can't Get Enough / Everything Counts*
Mute 1989

**Songs Of Faith And Devotion Live**: *I Feel You / Walking In My Shoes / Condemnation / Mercy In You / Judas / In Your Room / Get Right With Me / Rush / One Caress / Higher Love*
Mute 1993

**The Single 86>98**: Disc 1: *Stripped / A Question Of Lust / A Question Of Time*

/ *Strangelove* / *Never Let Me Down Again* / *Behind The Wheel* / *Personal Jesus* / *Enjoy The Silence* / *Policy Of Truth* / *World In My Eyes* Disc 2: *I Feel You* / *Walking In My Shoes* / *Condemnation* / *In Your Room* / *Barrel Of A Gun* / *It's No Good* / *Home* / *Useless* / *Only When I Lose Myself* / *Little 15* / *Everything Counts (Live)*.
Mute 1998

**Remixes 81-04**: Disc 1: *Never Let Me Down Again – Split Mix* / *Policy Of Truth – Capitol Mix* / *Shout – Rio Remix* / *Home – Air 'Around The Golf' Remix* / *Strangelove – Blind Mix* / *Rush – Spiritual Guidance Mix* / *I Feel You – Renegade Soundwave Afghan Surgery Mix* / *Barrel Of A Gun – Underworld Hard Mix* / *Route 66 – Beatmasters Mix* / *Freelove – DJ Muggs Remix* / *I Feel Loved – Chamber's Remix* / *Just Can't Get Enough – Schizo Mix*. Disc 2: *Personal Jesus – Pump Mix* / *World In My Eyes – Mode To Joy* / *Get The Balance Right! – Combination Mix* / *Everything Counts – Absolut Mix* / *Breathing In Fumes – Painkiller – Kill The Pain – DJ Shadow Vs. Depeche Mode* / *Useless – The Kruder + Dorfmeister Session™* / *In Your Room – The Jeep Rock Mix* / *Dream On – Dave Clarke Acoustic Version* / *It's No Good – Speedy J Mix* / *Master And Servant – An ON-USound Science Fiction Dance Hall Classic* / *Enjoy The Silence – Timo Maas Extended Remix*
Mute 2004

**The Best Of**: *Personal Jesus* / *Just Can't Get Enough* / *Everything Counts* / *Enjoy The Silence* / *Shake The Disease* / *See You* / *It's No Good* / *Strangelove* / *Suffer Well* / *Dream On* / *People Are People* / *Martyr* / *Walking In My Shoes* / *I Feel You* / *Precious* / *Master And Servant* / *New Life* / *Never Let Me Down Again*
Mute 2007

# SINGLES

**Dreaming Of Me**: *Dreaming Of Me / Ice Machine*
Mute seven inch 1981

**New Life**: *New Life / Shout*
Mute seven inch 1981

**Just Can't Get Enough**: *Just Can't Get Enough / Any Second Now*
Mute seven inch 1981

**See You**: *See You / Now, This Is Fun*
Mute seven inch 1982

**The Meaning Of Love**: *The Meaning Of Love / Oberkorn*
Mute seven inch 1982

**Leave In Silence**: *Leave In Silence / Excerpt From: My Secret Garden*
Mute seven inch 1982

**Get The Balance Right**: *Get The Balance Right / The Great Outdoors*
Mute seven inch 1983

**Everything Counts**: *Everything Counts / Work Hard*
Mute seven inch 1983

**Love, In Itself**: *Love, In Itself / Fools*
Mute seven inch 1983

**People Are People**: *People Are People / In Your Memory*
Mute seven inch 1984

**Master And Servant**: *Master & Servant / (Set Me Free) Remotivate Me*
Mute seven inch 1984

**Blasphemous Rumours / Somebody**: *Blasphemous Rumours / Somebody (Remix)*
Mute seven inch 1984

**Shake The Disease**: *Shake The Disease / Flexible*
Mute seven inch 1985

**It's Called A Heart**: *It's Called A Heart / Fly On The Windscreen*
Mute seven inch 1985

**Stripped / But Not Tonight**: *Stripped / But Not Tonight*
Mute seven inch 1986

**A Question Of Lust**: *A Question Of Lust / Christmas Island*
Mute seven inch 1986

**A Question Of Time**: *A Question Of Time (Remix) / Black Celebration (Live)*
Mute seven inch 1986

**Strangelove**: *Strangelove / Pimpf*
Mute seven inch 1987

**Never Let Me Down Again**: *Never Let Me Down Again / Pleasure, Little Treasure*
Mute seven inch 1987

**Behind The Wheel**: *Behind The Wheel (Remix) / Route 66*
Mute seven inch 1987

**Everything Counts (From 101):** *Everything Counts (Live) / Nothing (Live)*
Mute seven inch 1989

**Personal Jesus**: *Personal Jesus / Dangerous*
Mute seven inch 1989

**Enjoy The Silence**: *Enjoy The Silence / Memphisto*
Mute seven inch 1990

**Policy Of Truth**: *Policy Of Truth / Kaleid*
Mute seven inch 1990

**World In My Eyes**: *World In My Eyes (7 inch Version) / World In My Eyes (Oil Tank Mix) / Happiest Girl (Kiss-A-Mix) / Sea Of Sin (Tonal Mix)*
Mute CD single 1990

**I Feel You**: *I Feel You (Seven Inch Mix) / One Caress / I Feel You (Throb Mix) / I Feel You (Babylon Mix)*
Mute CD single 1993

**Walking In My Shoes**: *Walking In My Shoes (Seven Inch Mix) / Walking In My Shoes (Grungy Gonads Mix) / My Joy (Seven Inch Mix) / My Joy (Slow Slide Mix)*
Mute CD single 1993

**Condemnation**: *Condemnation (Paris Mix) / Death's Door (Jazz Mix) / Rush (Spiritual Guidance Mix) / Rush (Amylnitrate Mix [Instrumental])*
Mute CD single 1993

**In Your Room**: *In Your Room (Zephyr Mix) / In Your Room (Extended Zephyr*

Mix) / *Never Let Me Down Again (Live)* / *Death's Door (Live)*
Mute CD single 1994

**Barrel Of A Gun**: *Barrel Of A Gun / Painkiller / Barrel Of A Gun (Underworld Soft Mix) / Barrel Of A Gun (One Inch Punch Mix)*
Mute CD single 1997

**It's No Good**: *It's No Good / Slowblow (Darren Price Mix) / It's No Good (Bass Bounce Mix) / It's No Good (Speedy J Mix)*
Mute CD single 1997

**Home**: *Home (Jedi Knights Remix [Drowning In Time] / Home (Grantby Mix) / Barrel Of A Gun (Live) / It's No Good (Live)*
Mute CD single 1997

**Useless**: *Useless (Remix) / Useless (Escape From Wherever: Parts 1 & 2!) / Useless (Cosmic Blues Mix) / Barrel Of A Gun (Video)*
Mute CD single 1997

**Only When I Lose Myself**: *Only When I Lose Myself / Surrender / Headstar*
Mute CD single 1998

**Dream On**: *Dream On (Single Version) / Easy Tiger (Full Version) / Easy Tiger (Bertrand Burgalat & A.S Dragon Version)*
Mute CD single 2001

**I Feel Loved**: *I Feel Loved (Single Version) / Dirt (Single Version) / I Feel Loved (Extended Instrumental)*
Mute CD single 2001

**Freelove**: *Freelove (Flood Mix) / Zenstation / Zenstation (Atom's Stereonerd Remix)*
Mute CD single 2001

**Goodnight Lovers**: *Goodnight Lovers / When The Body Speaks (Acoustic Version) / The Dead Of Night (Electronicat Remix) / Goodnight Lovers (Falling Leaf Mix)*
Mute CD single 2002

**Enjoy The Silence 04**: *Enjoy The Silence (Reinterpreted by Mike Shinoda) / Halo (Goldfrapp Remix)*
Mute CD single 2004

**Precious**: *Precious (Album Version) / Precious (Sasha's Spooky Mix – Single Edit)*
Mute CD single 2005

**A Pain That I'm Used To**: *A Pain That I'm Used To / Newborn*
Mute CD single 2005

**Suffer Well**: *Suffer Well / Better Days*
Mute CD single 2006

**John The Revelator / Lilian**: *John The Revelator (Single Version) / Lilian (Single Version)*
Mute CD single 2006

**Martyr**: *Martyr (Single Version) / Martyr (Booka Shade Vocal)*
Mute CD single 2006

# DAVE GAHAN DISCOGRAPHY
## ALBUMS

**Paper Monsters**: *Dirty Sticky Floors / Hold On / A Little Piece / Bottle Living / Black And Blue Again / Stay / I Need You / Bitter Apple / Hidden Houses / Goodbye*
Mute 2003

**Hourglass**: *Saw Something / Kingdom / Deeper and Deeper / 21 Days / Miracles / Use You / Insoluble / Endless / A Little Lie / Down*
Mute 2007

COMPILATIONS

**Soundtrack To Live Monsters**: *Hidden Houses / Hold On / Dirty Sticky Floors / Bitter Apple / Black and Blue Again / Stay / A Little Piece / I Need You / Bottle Living / Goodbye*
Mute Digital Download 2004

**Live From SoHo**: *Saw Something / Kingdom / Deeper And Deeper / Use You / Endless / A Little Lie / Miracles*
Mute Digital Download through iTunes 2007

SINGLES

**Dirty Sticky Floors**: *Dirty Sticky Floors / Stand Up / Maybe*
Mute CD single 2003

**I Need You**: *I Need You (Radio Mix) / Closer (Single Version) / Breathe (Single Version)*
Mute CD single 2003

**Bottle Living / Hold On**: *Bottle Living (Album Version) / Hold On (Radio Mix – Extended Version) / Bottle Living (Tomcraft Vocal)*
Mute CD single 2003

**A Little Piece**: *A Little Piece (live at the Olympia, Paris)*
Mute digital download single 2004

**Kingdom**: *Kingdom (Single version) / Tomorrow*
Mute CD single 2007

**Saw Something / Deeper And Deeper**: *Saw Something (Single version) / Deeper and Deeper (Shrubbn!! single version) / Love Will Leave (Das Shadow's rewerk) / Deeper and Deeper (Juan MacLean club mix)*
Mute single 2007

Visit our website at *www.impbooks.com*
for more information on our full list
of titles including books on:

Thom Yorke, Bernard Sumner, MC5, Bruce Dickinson,
Slash, 'Skins', 'Scooter Boys', Dave Grohl, Muse,
Richard Ashcroft, Green Day, Ian Hunter, Mick Ronson,
David Bowie, The Killers, My Chemical Romance,
System Of A Down, The Prodigy and many more.